AF572114

AMERICAN ART

Paintings from the Amon Carter Museum

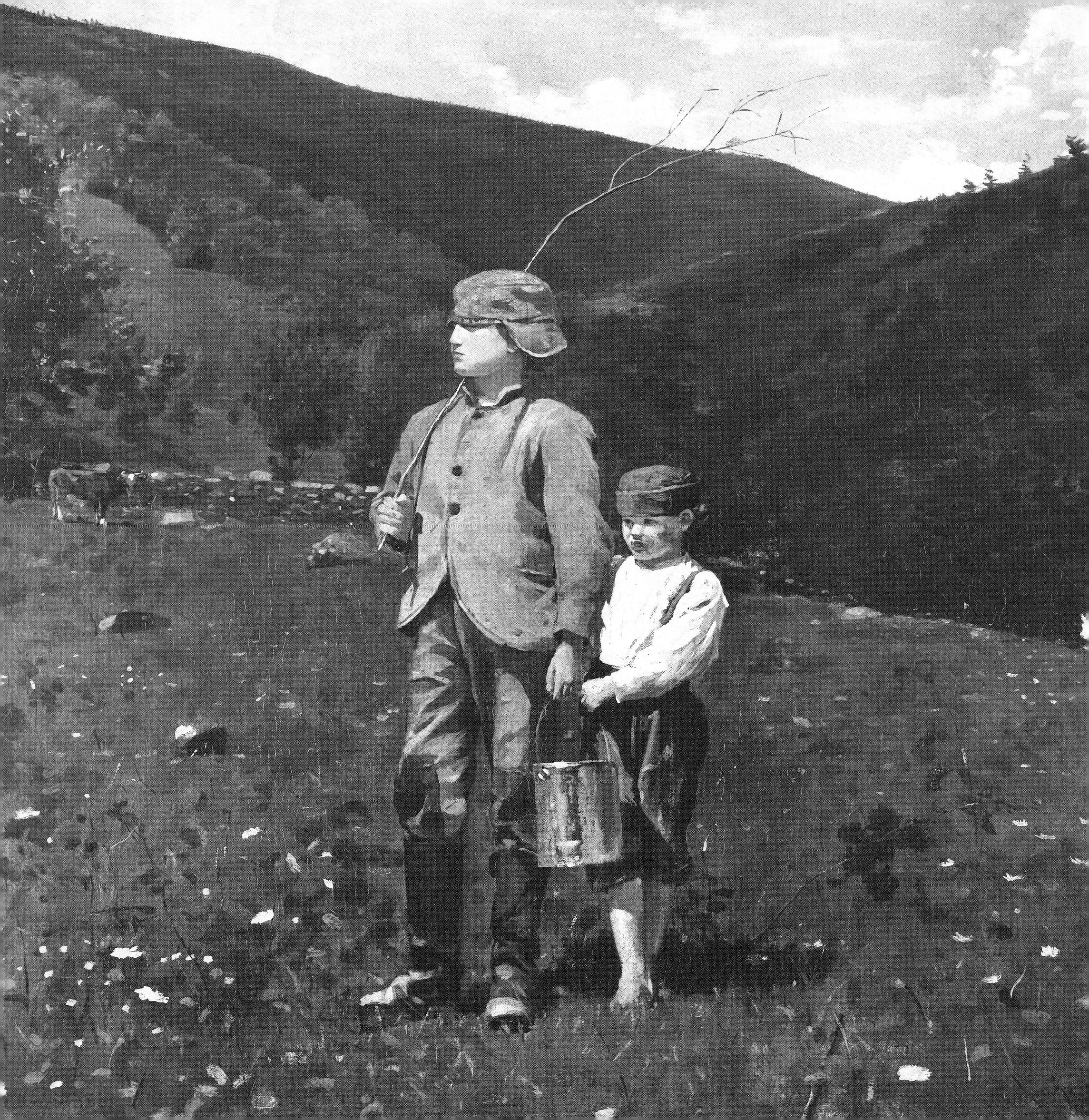

AMERICAN ART

Paintings from the Amon Carter Museum

SARAH CASH

Assistant Curator, Amon Carter Museum

AMON CARTER MUSEUM

Fort Worth, Texas

Distributed by the Amon Carter Museum, Fort Worth

ISBN 0-88360-070-6
LC 92-54538

Design by DUO Design Group, Inc., Fort Worth, Texas
Color separations by JTM Colorscan, Inc., Fort Worth, Texas
Printing by Jarvis Press, Dallas, Texas

Frontispiece: Detail of Winslow Homer, *Crossing the Pasture*, c. 1872, oil on canvas
This page: Photograph by Luther Smith

INTRODUCTION

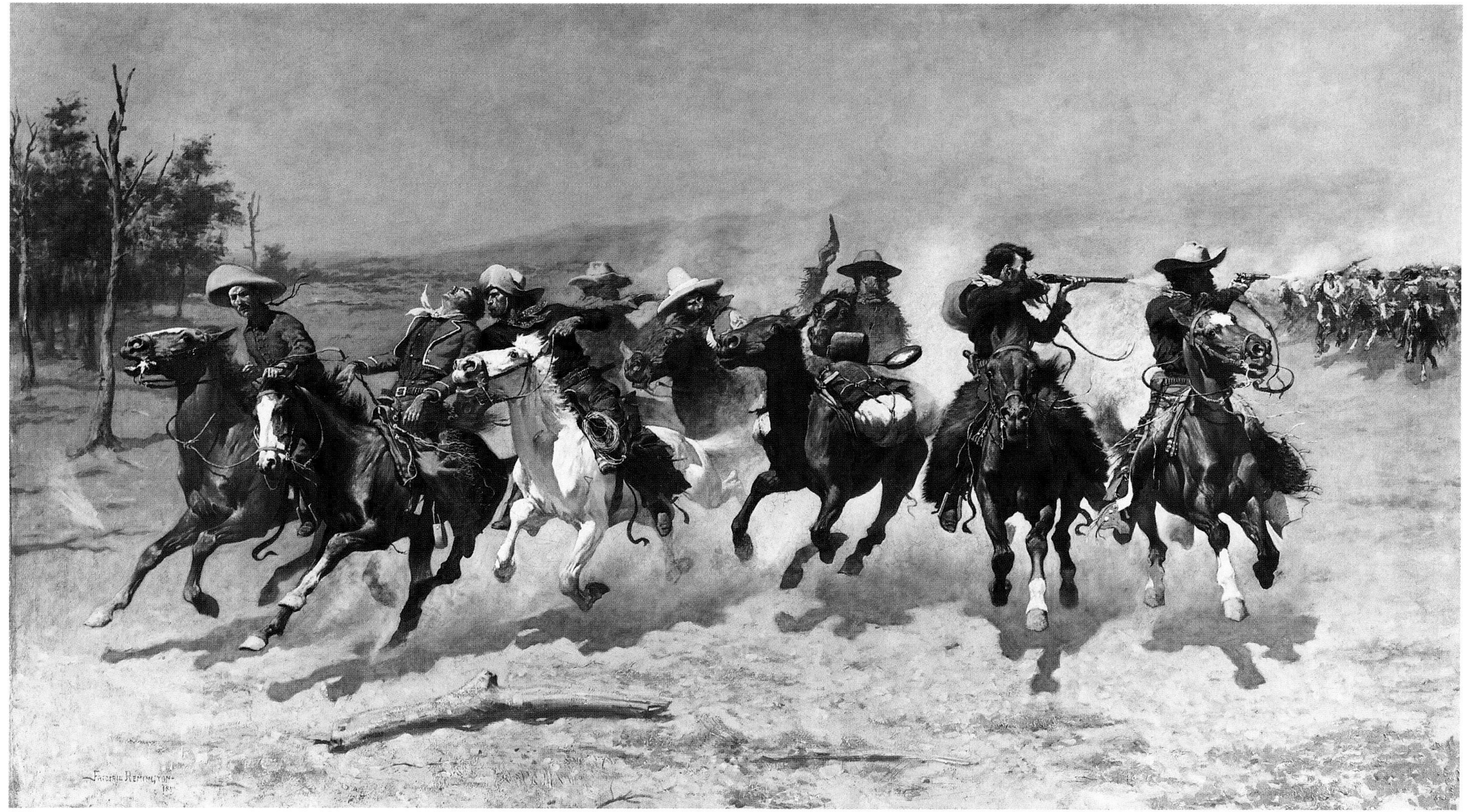

Frederic Remington, *A Dash for the Timber*, 1889, oil on canvas

This book highlights a selection of twenty-five paintings acquired by the Amon Carter Museum since it opened its doors in 1961. The Museum was established through the will of Amon G. Carter, Sr. (1879–1955), a Fort Worth businessman, oilman, communications pioneer, and publisher of the *Fort Worth Star-Telegram* as well as a leader in the development of his city and the West Texas region. Carter envisioned a public arena for the exhibition of his rich and extensive collection of over four hundred works by Frederic Remington and Charles M. Russell. It was to be an "artistic enterprise" for the benefit of all, and he hoped that its collections and programs would "particularly stimulate artistic imagination among young people."

The Museum's building was designed by noted architect Philip Johnson to house Carter's collection of Western art, which is still prominently featured and includes such masterpieces as Remington's cinematic canvas *A Dash for the Timber* (1889) and his 1895 bronze *The Bronco Buster*, as well as Russell's colorful *A Tight Dally and a Loose Latigo* of 1920. Almost immediately, the view of the West represented in the inaugural collection was enriched by additional acquisitions and by exhibitions and publications which encouraged the study of "westering North America," including European, Mexican, and Canadian artists' chronicles and celebrations of the settlement of the continent. The

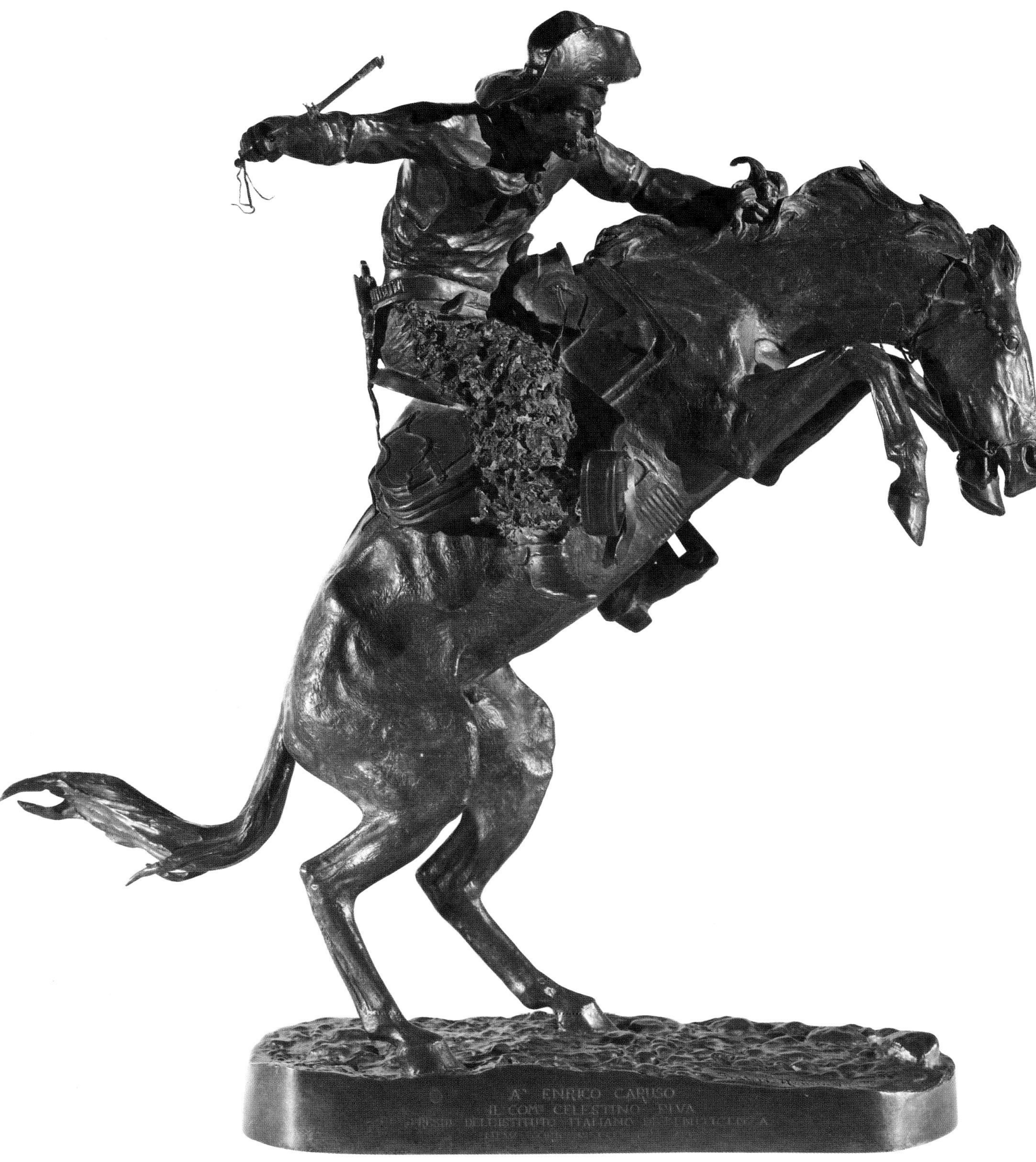

Frederic Remington, *The Bronco Buster*, 1906, bronze

building was expanded in 1964 and again in 1977 to accommodate the Museum's growing collections and programs.

As the Museum began to collect paintings, sculpture, prints, watercolors, and drawings by artists whose work exemplified the most important artistic achievements in the United States from about 1825 to 1960, these holdings were soon placed in the broader context of the history of North America's art and culture. Photographs were added to the collection from the outset; photographer Dorothea Lange gave the Museum its first photograph—her portrait of Charles M. Russell—the year the Museum opened. Since 1980 photography has played a critical role in the Museum's overall program, and today there are over 300,000 prints and negatives in the collection, including the photographic estates of such important artists as Laura Gilpin and Eliot Porter. In all media, works of art have been added to the collection not only for their high artistic quality and notable historical significance, but also for their interpretive potential. Each one illuminates aspects of American life and art; taken together, they represent a wide range of creative ideas and issues.

There are now over three hundred paintings in the Museum's collection. These include comprehensive representations by Remington and Russell, as well as a selective survey of nineteenth- and early twentieth-century American art. The collection features a few artistic movements in some depth—landscapes by the Hudson River School painters and still lifes by the trompe-l'oeil school of painters are most notable—and certain artists, such as Carl Wimar, Thomas Cole, Martin Johnson Heade, William M. Harnett, Georgia O'Keeffe, and Arthur Dove, are represented by multiple examples. Thus, while the Museum might easily be viewed on a single occasion, its riches and depth reward the returning visitor, especially when its holdings are viewed in the context of the complementary collections of the neighboring Kimbell Art Museum and Modern Art Museum of Fort Worth.

The Museum's growing sculpture collection features outstanding modernist works by such artists as Robert Laurent and Elie Nadelman to complement its fine paintings from that period, as well as Augustus Saint-Gaudens' majestic *Diana*

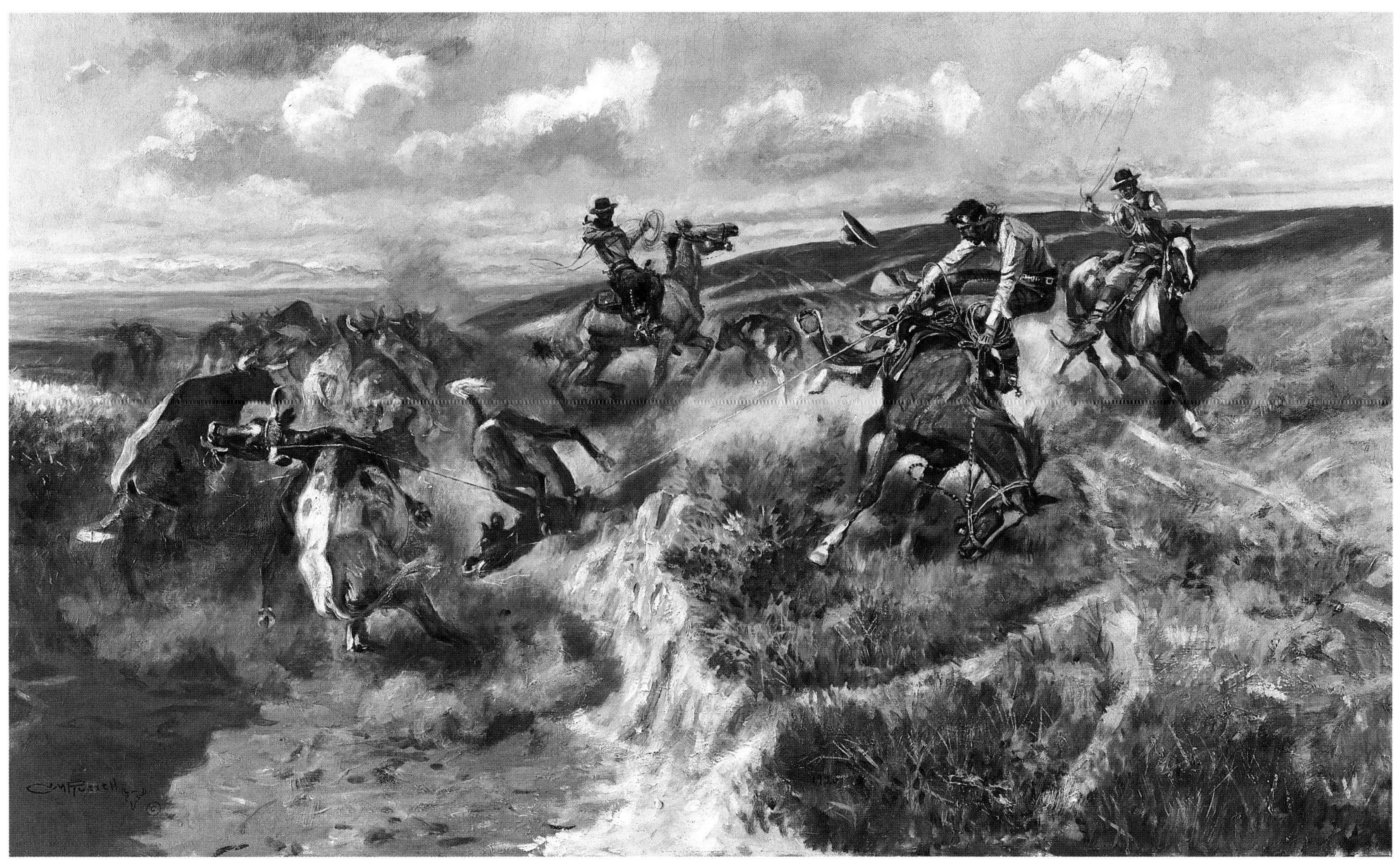

Charles M. Russell, *A Tight Dally and a Loose Latigo*, 1920, oil on canvas (modeled in 1892–94, cast in 1928). These pieces join the exemplary selection of Remington and Russell bronzes, as well as Russell's wax sculptures, included in Amon Carter's original collection, and form the foundation of a survey of American sculpture that is planned to parallel the Museum's collection of paintings.

Augmenting the paintings and sculpture are over six hundred drawings and watercolors and more than five thousand prints, ranging from historical works (such as city views and early scenes by artist-explorers), to wildlife studies, landscapes, and early modernist imagery. In addition, the Amon Carter Museum's library collects and exhibits fine illustrated books. These works, like selections from the photography collection, are exhibited in rotation, as their paper supports and fragile media do not permit sustained exposure to light.

As it moves toward the twenty-first century, the Amon Carter Museum remains committed to its mission to collect, preserve, exhibit, and foster a better understanding and appreciation of American art. The Museum's rich collection, reflecting many aspects of American art and culture, will remain accessible to the public through installations of the permanent collection, temporary exhibitions, publications, and educational programs in order to fulfill Amon Carter's dream of an institution dedicated to enriching the lives of Fort Worth's residents and its visitors.

Opposite page: Augustus Saint-Gaudens, *Diana*, 1928, gilded bronze

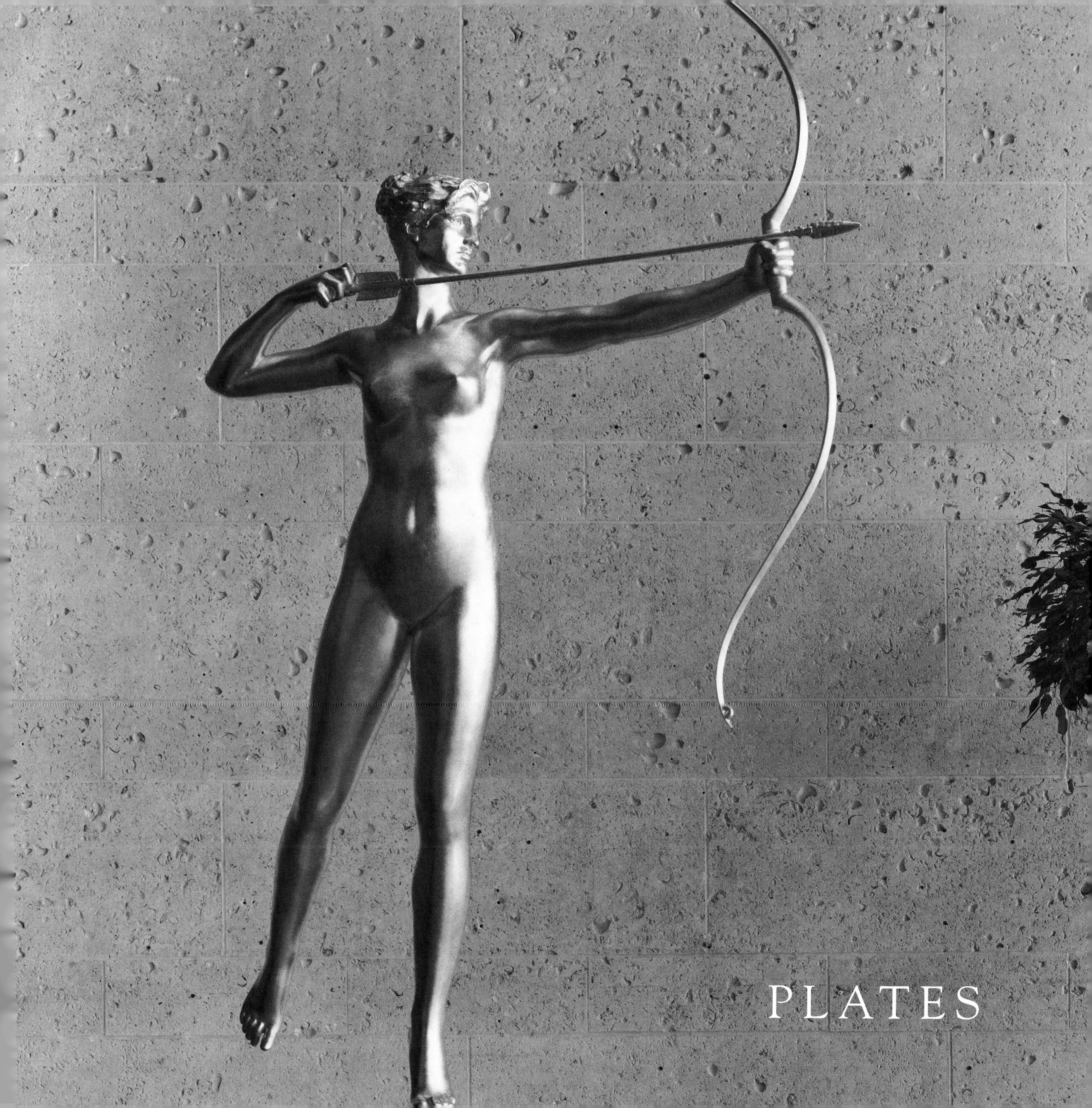

PLATES

THOMAS COLE
(1801–1848)

The Garden of Eden

1828
Oil on canvas, 38½ x 52¾ in.
(97.8 x 134 cm)

Immensely successful as the first painter to champion the national landscape, Thomas Cole greatly influenced the course of nineteenth-century American art. Landscape painting before his time was considered inferior to religious and historical genres, but he won recognition for his landscapes and inspired two generations of artists, collectively known as the Hudson River School.

Little in Cole's early training anticipated this major accomplishment. Following an apprenticeship with an engraver in his native England, he arrived in the United States with his family at age seventeen and trained briefly at the Pennsylvania Academy of the Fine Arts. By the time he began *The Garden of Eden*, the artist already had settled in New York, where he earned recognition for works inspired by his first trip to the Hudson River Valley.

Although his followers generally would advocate an art of "pure" landscape, Cole himself preferred to enhance realism with idealization and to instruct his viewers through religious or moral references incorporated into his paintings. *The Garden of Eden* is an early masterpiece that exemplifies this approach. The diminutive Adam and Eve are depicted in a tropical, verdant Eden which, although largely imaginary, is set against a view of New Hampshire's Mount Chocorua. Certain elements of the composition were inspired by John Milton's *Paradise Lost*, and others suggest Cole's familiarity with works by the Flemish painter Jan Brueghel (1568–1625) and the English artist John Martin (1789–1854).

While the painting depicts a biblical subject, its underlying theme is the widely held view of America as the modern Garden of Eden, where man lives in harmony with unspoiled nature. Cole and his contemporaries perceived the nation's fertile landscape as the embodiment of divine presence and took care to paint its every detail, as in the delicately rendered flora and fauna.

The Garden of Eden and its pendant, *Expulsion from the Garden of Eden* (1828, Museum of Fine Arts, Boston), comprise the artist's first use of sequential imagery, foretelling his ambitious cycles such as *The Voyage of Life* (1840, Munson-Williams-Proctor Institute) and *The Course of Empire* (1836, New-York Historical Society). Although neither of Cole's paintings sold when he exhibited them at New York's prestigious National Academy of Design in 1828, within a year he had found buyers for each. *The Garden of Eden* was displayed again at the National Academy in 1831 and engraved the same year as a frontispiece for a Boston edition of the Bible, then disappeared from public view until 1990, when it entered the Amon Carter Museum collection.

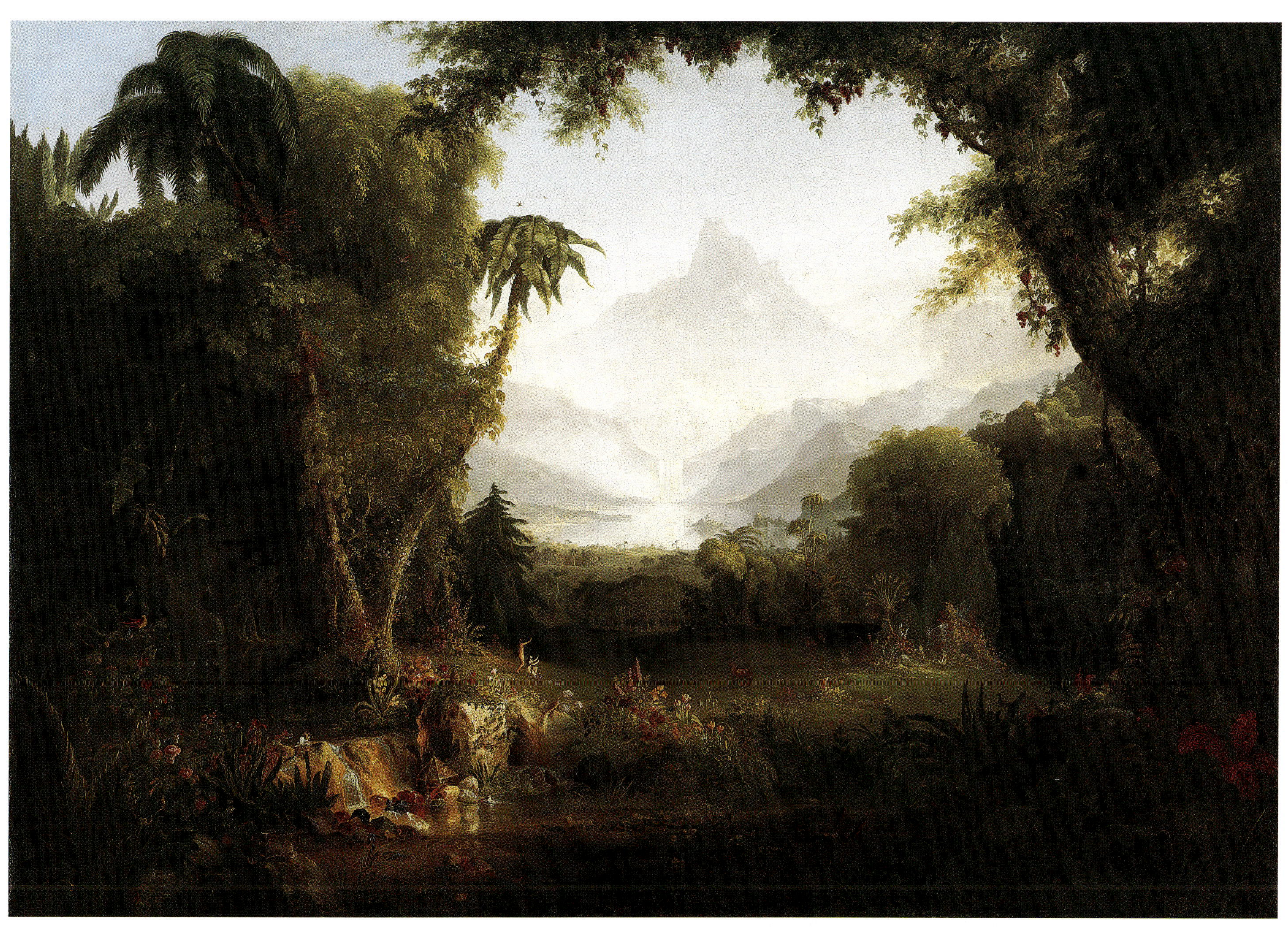

THOMAS COLE
(1801–1848)

The Hunter's Return

1845
Oil on canvas, 40⅛ x 60½ in.
(101.9 x 153.7 cm)

The Hunter's Return invites comparison with *The Garden of Eden*, Cole's canvas of seventeen years earlier (see preceding plate). Both scenes include New Hampshire's majestic Mount Chocorua, which Cole sketched in the late 1820s on one of his many trips through New England from his home in New York. However, the largely fantastic setting of *The Garden of Eden*, with its ethereal clouds, mist, and waterfalls, has been replaced in *The Hunter's Return* with a more realistic landscape. The later painting incorporates narrative elements in the foreground, reflecting Cole's desire to elevate landscape to what he called "a higher style of art."

Cole may have had a personal inspiration for this scene. After he moved to Catskill, New York, in 1836, his frequent sketching trips and business in New York City took him away from home for extended periods. *The Hunter's Return* may reflect the spirit of his own family's joyful reunions—an interpretation reinforced by the prominent position of Cole's signature under the hunter.

The New World remains Edenic in this contemporary scene, which shows man living harmoniously with nature in her late-day autumnal beauty. However, the remnants of cleared trees in the painting's foreground also warn the American public that it could "fall from grace" by destroying the wilderness in the name of settlement and progress.

Like *The Garden of Eden*, *The Hunter's Return* disappeared from public view for well over one hundred years before its rediscovery. Viewed together, the two works provide fine complementary examples of Cole's early and mature works. Moreover, as excellent representations of Cole's subject matter and style, they help to illuminate his influence on other Hudson River School artists, whose work is well represented in the Museum's collection.

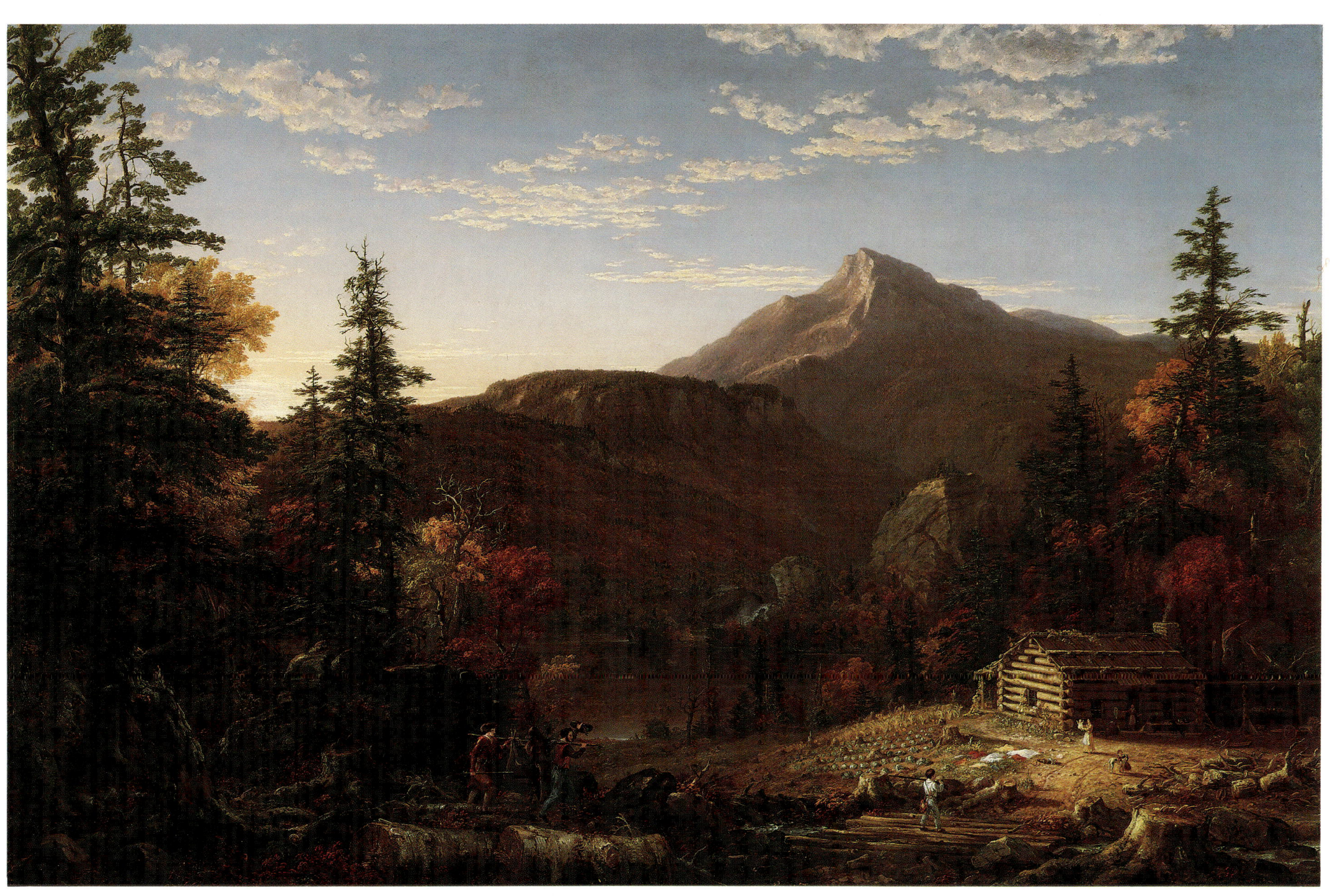

FREDERIC EDWIN CHURCH
(1826–1900)

New England Landscape (Evening After a Storm)

c. 1849
Oil on canvas, 25⅛ x 36¼ in.
(63.8 x 92.1 cm)

From his auspicious beginnings as Thomas Cole's first pupil, Frederic Church came to succeed his teacher as nineteenth-century America's foremost landscape painter. Early in his career, he achieved recognition for his tight draughtsmanship and crisp style of painting and was elected to full membership in the National Academy of Design at the age of twenty-three. At about this time, a few years after his two-year study with Cole, Church painted *New England Landscape*. The canvas shows the younger artist's absorption of his teacher's subject matter, compositional and technical formulas, and palette. Following Cole's frequent practice, Church combined several different views of New England scenery—probably Vermont's—based on sketches made during summer trips. The peaceful scene, blanketed by a sky breaking after a storm, represents the "new Eden" that the Hudson River School artists treated so frequently in their landscapes.

While it clearly relies upon Cole's example, *New England Landscape* also reveals Church's emerging personal style. He minimizes the overt narrative of the older artist's works—such as *The Hunter's Return* (see preceding plate), painted while Church studied with Cole—in favor of a quiet view that invites the observer to contemplate its simple, yet varied, beauty. Passages such as the picnic scene at the lower left and the exquisitely painted reflections on the water's surface are crafted with the meticulous detail that became a hallmark of Church's mature work. The artist's masterful rendering of atmospheric effects, for which he was also known, can be seen in the delicate mist above the water and in the breaking clouds that recede into a purple haze in the background. His use of light, although not as dramatic as it would become later in his career, delineates objects more clearly than does Cole's. In all of these aspects, the painting anticipates Church's masterpiece titled *New England Scenery* (1851, George Walter Vincent Smith Art Museum, Springfield, Massachusetts).

New England Landscape is a fine example of Church's early, tranquil landscapes, which were soon to be supplanted by large-scale, epic canvases documenting his travels in North and South America, the West Indies, Europe, and the Near East. These later works, often depicting natural wonders such as Niagara Falls or the Andes mountains, were exhibited to great critical acclaim in the late 1850s and the 1860s, securing Church's fame. Toward the end of his life, however, public taste turned away from his grand, nationalistic style of painting. As artistic fashion moved toward more intimate scenes inspired by French Barbizon art, the aging artist devoted himself to the design and construction of his grand home Olana, set high above the banks of the Hudson River that had inspired many of his landscapes.

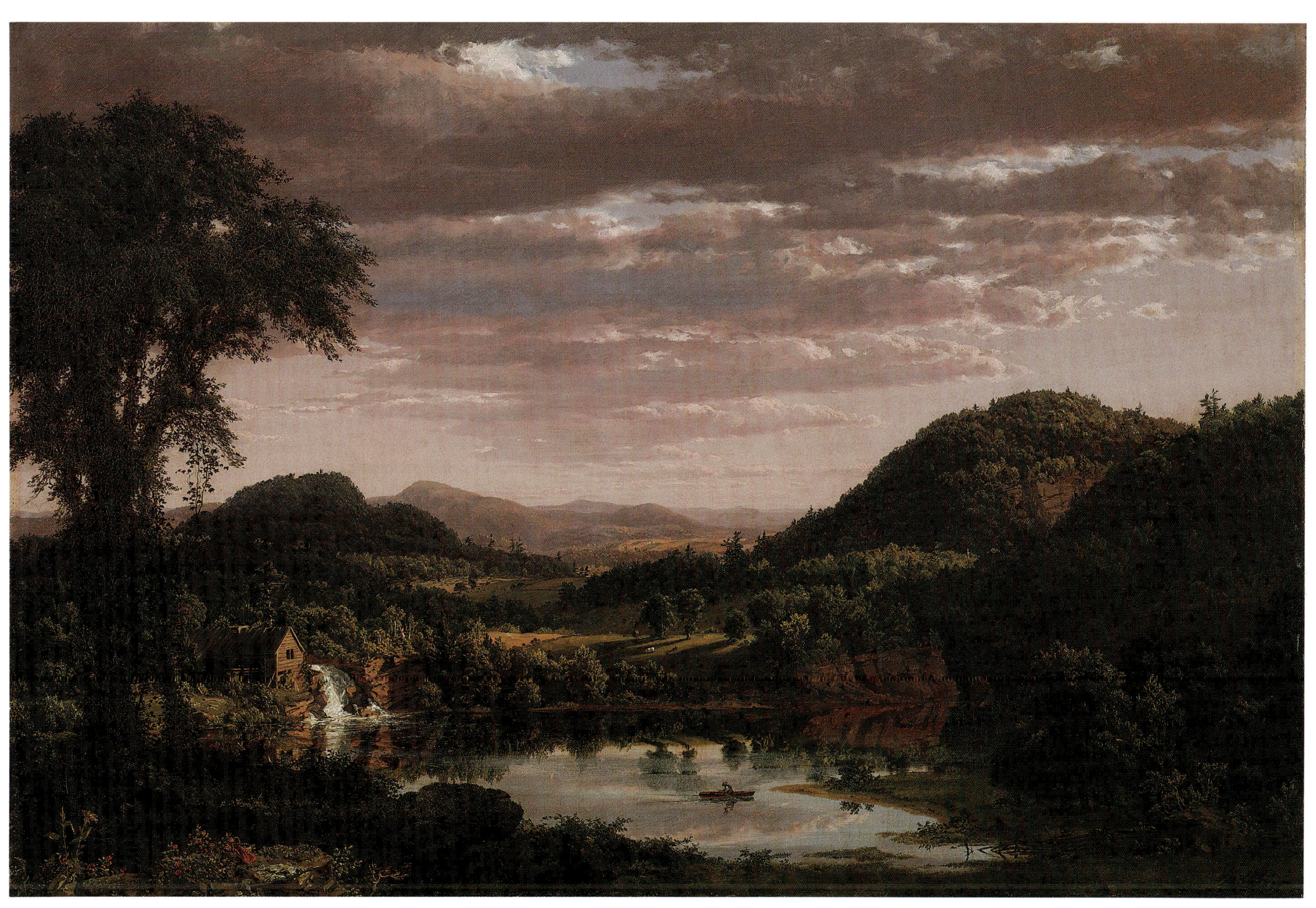

JOHN MIX STANLEY
(1814–1872)

Oregon City on the Willamette River

c. 1850–52
Oil on canvas, 26½ x 40 in.
(67.3 x 101.6 cm)

After working as a sign painter, a coach maker, and an itinerant portraitist in his native New York State, John Mix Stanley in 1839 began a fifteen-year period of travel throughout the West and Southwest in order to paint portraits of Indians from various tribes. Returning to the East, he displayed most of these works as a traveling Indian Gallery until they were destroyed by a fire at the Smithsonian Institution in 1865. Consequently, Stanley is now better known as an artist of western landscapes and genre scenes, including *Oregon City on the Willamette River* and *Scene on the Colorado River* (Amon Carter Museum, c. 1852).

In 1847, Stanley left his work as a topographical artist on a military expedition to California to undertake a one-thousand-mile journey through the Oregon Territory. On this trip he conceived this picturesque view of Oregon City on the Willamette River. While certainly sketched on site in the winter of 1848, the painting was likely completed after the artist returned to the East in 1850, following travels that included a year in Hawaii.

The simple rendering of the city's orderly frame houses and church recalls Stanley's background as a sign painter, but he employs traditional landscape practice by framing the scene with a tree and knoll at the left. The clear, warm sunlight that falls on the town is puncuated by the shadows of passing clouds in the broad expanse of sky. Despite the town's calm and idyllic appearance in this painting, Oregon City at midcentury was home to a growing lumber industry, evidenced in the several sawmills to the left of the falls. The Oregon Treaty of 1846 gave the United States claim to the Pacific Northwest, and to acknowledge that the Willamette Falls Indians were losing their native lands to the settlers' lumber and fishing enterprises, Stanley depicts two Indians turning away from the settlement.

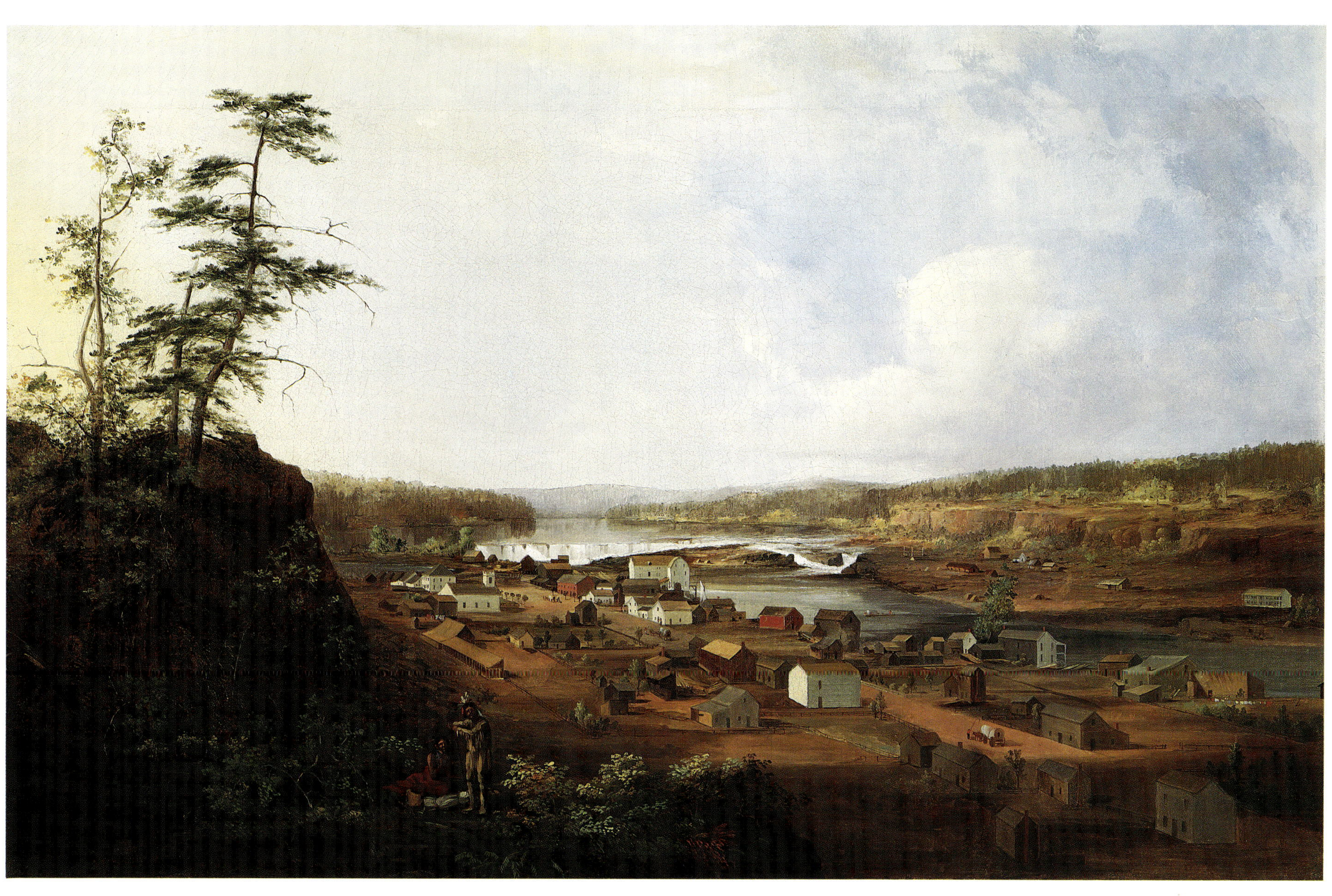

SETH EASTMAN
(1808–1875)

Ballplay of the Sioux on the St. Peters River in Winter

1848
Oil on canvas, 25¾ x 35¼ in.
(65.4 x 89.5 cm)
Acquisition in memory of Mitchell A. Wilder, Director, Amon Carter Museum, 1961–1979

Seth Eastman's works portray almost every aspect of ordinary life among Plains Indian tribes, making him, after George Catlin, one of the best-known painters of native Americans during the first half of the nineteenth century. Born in Brunswick, Maine, Eastman studied topographical drawing at West Point, then served in the army for thirty years. It was at his frontier posts in Wisconsin, Minnesota, Florida, and Texas that Eastman developed his interest in the American Indian.

Ballplay of the Sioux is among the finest of over four hundred paintings, watercolors, and drawings of Indian life and the Minnesota landscape that Eastman created during his second tour of military service at Fort Snelling, Minnesota, from 1841 to 1848. The Indians' fast-paced and often violent ball game, a forerunner of present-day lacrosse, provided excellent combat training. Eastman's winter setting, with its bare trees and rose-gray sky, is somewhat unusual; the game was traditionally played on an open plain during the summer, but he shows a match on the frozen St. Peters River (now the Minnesota River) near the fort. Often, one Indian village would challenge another, and the match could involve several hundred players.

Eastman has carefully detailed the elaborate, colorful costumes of the main participants. As his wife Mary, herself a chronicler of Indian life, noted, the Sioux wore their "choicest finery" for the game. The still-life elements seen in the left foreground, including weapons, clothing, cooking utensils, and buffalo robes, may well have been items wagered on the game's outcome. The expressive faces and graceful stances of the players and spectators are a particularly engaging aspect of this picturesque document of Sioux leisure.

Eastman treated this subject in at least one other canvas, an 1851 version at the Corcoran Gallery of Art, Washington, D.C. Another rendering of the game appeared as one of the many illustrations that Eastman completed while in Washington, D.C., between frontier postings; these were engraved for Henry R. Schoolcraft's six-volume study of the North American Indian, published between 1851 and 1857. Eastman continued to pursue his interest in Indian life and customs even after completing his military duty; during the last years of his life he painted canvases depicting Indian scenes and views of American forts for the U.S. Capitol building.

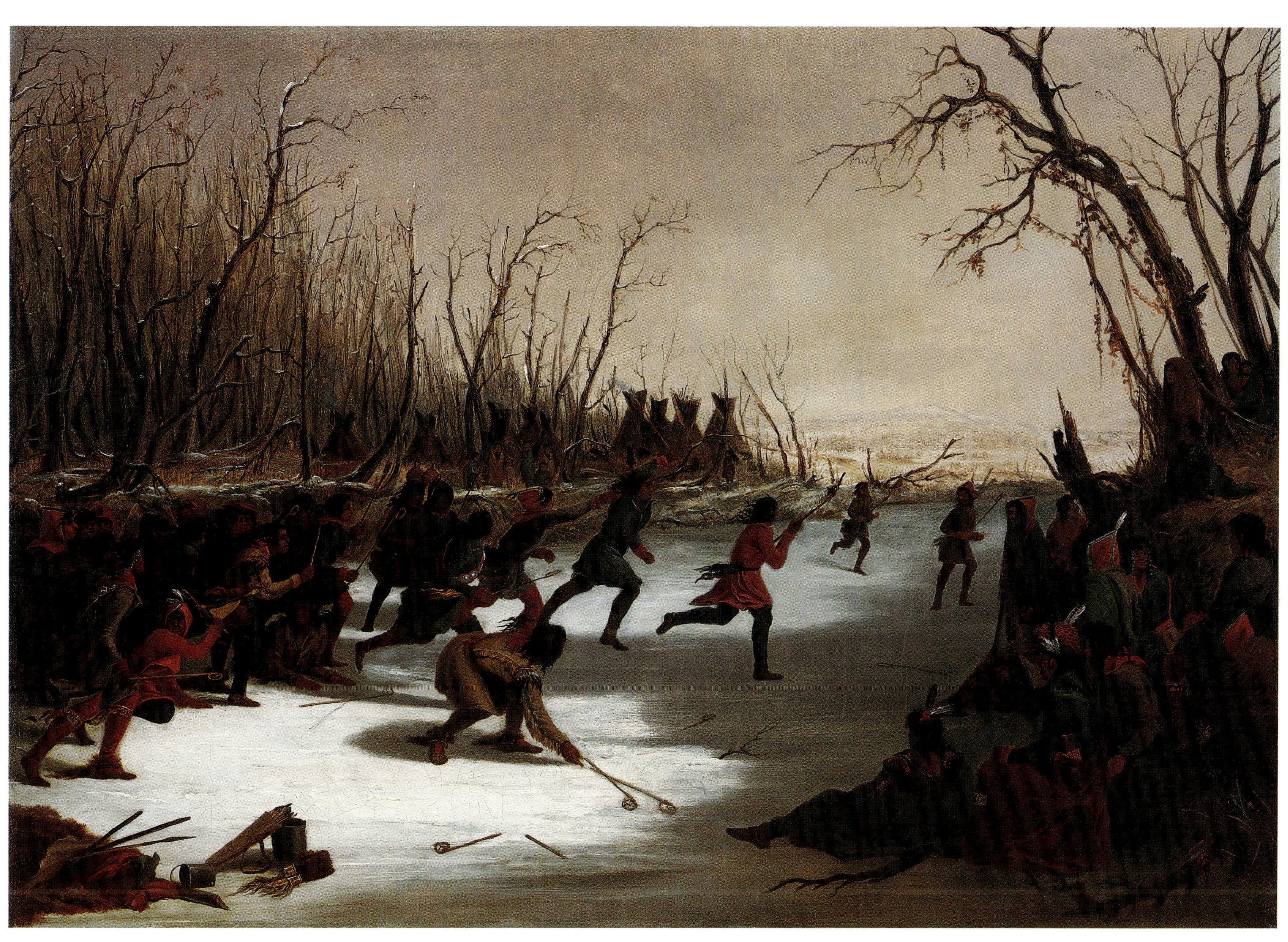

FITZ HUGH LANE
(1804–1865)

Boston Harbor

1856
Oil on canvas, 25½ x 42¼ in.
(64.8 x 107.3 cm)

Fitz Hugh Lane, one of the foremost marine painters of nineteenth-century America, specialized in topographically detailed yet poetic and light-filled harbor and coastal scenes. Distinctive of his hand, this lyrical, contemplative view of Boston Harbor reveals his skilled draughtsmanship—a result of his early training in a Boston lithography shop. Though Lane lived in the city only during the 1830s and 1840s, he painted its harbor throughout most of his career. The artist returned to his native Gloucester in 1849 and, except for a few painting trips to Maine, remained there for the rest of his life.

Stylistically, *Boston Harbor* falls between the artist's earlier, more strictly topographical harbor views and his late, lyrical scenes in which human presence is eliminated. The meticulously rendered geographical and nautical details demonstrate the artist's familiarity with the Boston area and its great variety of shipping activity. To suggest the country's rapid industrialization during this period—a theme that other artists represented in railroad subjects—Lane's scene includes a powerful steamship cutting a wake between the becalmed clippers. While paintings such as *Boston Harbor* were clearly inspired by Lane's surroundings, they also reflect his awareness of seventeenth-century Dutch harbor views and the Boston marine views of his near contemporary, British-born Robert Salmon.

Boston Harbor is characteristic of Lane's interest in accurately rendering the light and atmosphere of a locale. Most nineteenth-century American landscapists shared this proclivity, but Lane and his contemporaries, including Martin Johnson Heade, Frederic Edwin Church, and John Frederick Kensett—sometimes referred to as the luminists—cultivated this quality most fully during the third quarter of the nineteenth century. The radiant light, visible atmosphere, horizontality, and scant human presence in *Boston Harbor* coalesce to create a still, peaceful scene. Furthering the work's sense of placidity is its thinly painted surface, in which all brushwork is obscured. Like the earlier Hudson River School painters, Lane and other luminists used their works to express strong nationalistic pride as well as religious overtones. These artists saw the hand of God embodied not only in the wondrous variety of nature but even more fully in the pure, clear light which dominated their style.

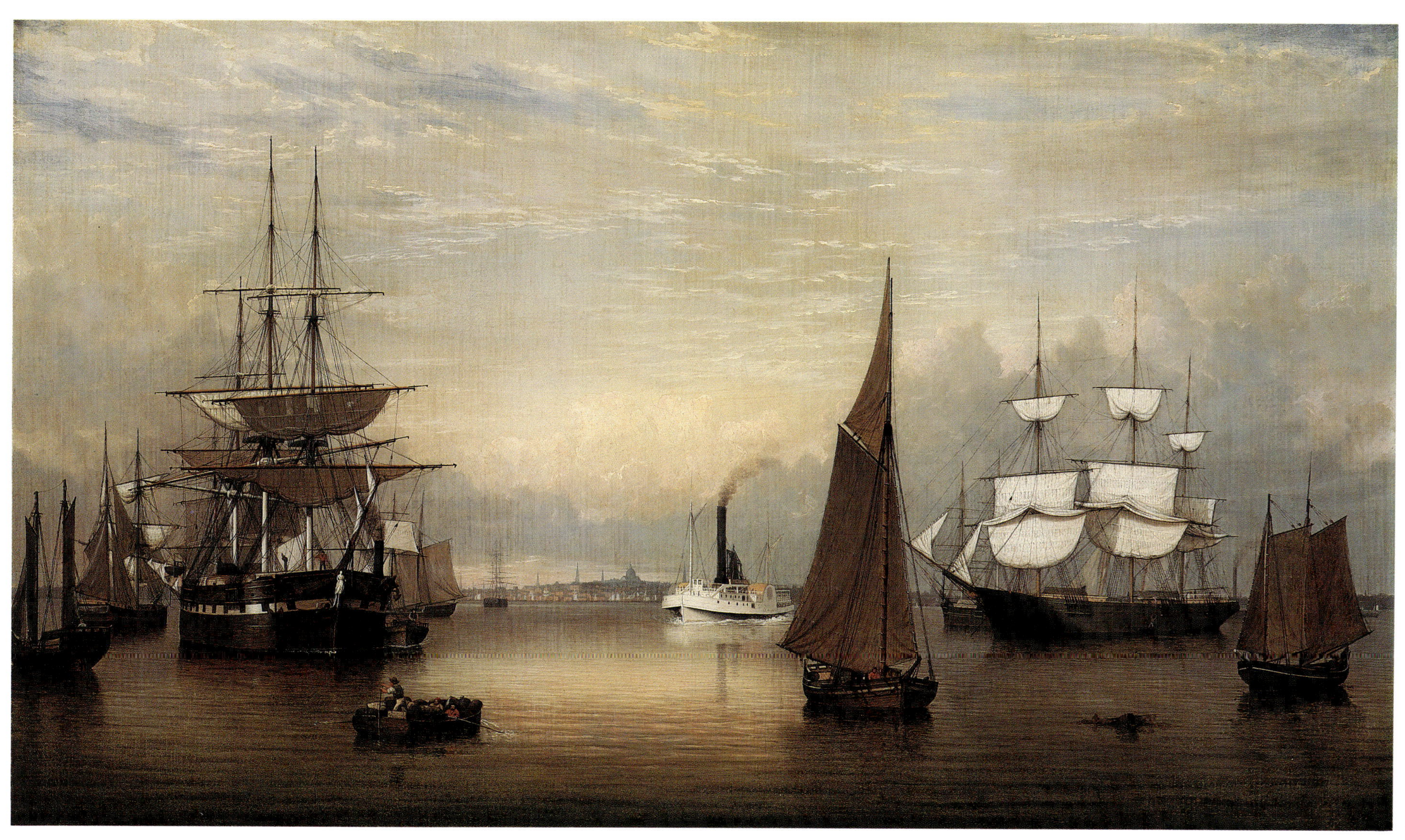

MARTIN JOHNSON HEADE
(1819–1904)

Thunderstorm Over Narragansett Bay

1868
Oil on canvas, 32⅛ x 54½ in.
(81.6 x 138.4 cm)

Martin Johnson Heade excelled in both landscape and still-life painting, yet he remains one of the nineteenth century's most enigmatic artists. Although he achieved modest success as a portraitist in his native Bucks County, Pennsylvania, and painted in Rome, Heade was never fully accepted in the official art world and was largely forgotten near the end of his life. This was due in part to his unusual subjects—salt marshes, hummingbirds and orchids in their natural surroundings, and the occasional representation of a thunderstorm. Yet the rediscovery of his dramatic *Thunderstorm Over Narragansett Bay* in the early 1940s immediately renewed interest in the artist and his work; the painting's eerie intensity especially appealed to a public familiar with surrealist works being produced in America at that time. Now recognized as the masterpiece of his long career, the painting is a unique synthesis of a romanticized subject with tightly painted detail.

Heade's interest in the changing effects of light and weather on the landscape led him, in the 1860s, to begin painting coastal scenes in the Northeast. The horizontality and the emphasis on light and atmospheric effects in *Thunderstorm Over Narragansett Bay* can also be found in landscape views created by his contemporaries, but Heade developed a highly personal and distinctive vision. He has manipulated a natural meteorological effect, the glow created by sunlight raking under storm clouds, to dramatic advantage. The graceful sailboats, some nearing safety and some of uncertain destiny, all seem calm in the face of the breaking storm. The tiny figures, struggling to lower sails and carry gear to safety, are likewise powerless under the threatening sky. The contrast of light sails and shore against dark sea and sky, the clarity of detail, and the almost frozen, airless quality of the painting help make the scene apparitional and unsettling.

It is not coincidental that Heade's thunderstorm paintings and similarly apocalyptic works by other artists were created during the tumultuous decade of the Civil War. Just as the tranquil landscapes of the Hudson River School symbolize man's harmonious coexistence with nature earlier in the century, so these images of thunderstorms, dramatic sunsets, and ravaged nature are metaphors for the most divisive and destructive event in the young nation's history. When *Thunderstorm Over Narragansett Bay* was exhibited at the Brooklyn Art Association in 1868, however, its contemporary relevance was eclipsed by its intense and unprecedented visual effects. The painting was not well received at the time, but today its beauty, mystery, and sheer technical mastery confirm its status as one of the Museum's finest paintings.

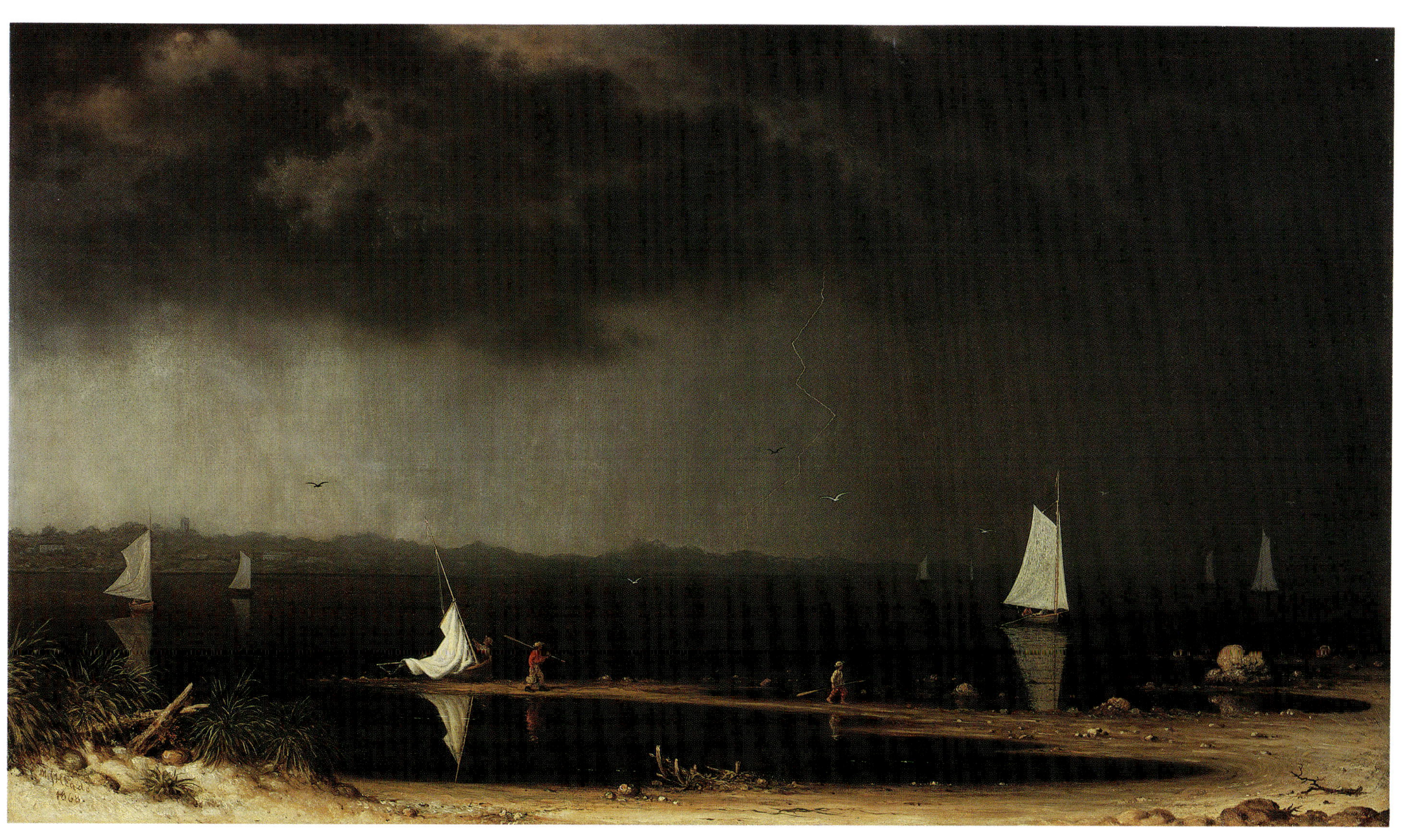

MARTIN JOHNSON HEADE
(1819–1904)

Marshfield Meadows, Massachusetts

1870s
Oil on canvas, 17⅛ x 36¼ in.
(43.5 x 92.1 cm)

Martin Johnson Heade's mature career is distinguished by his recurrent and prolific treatment of three subjects: cut flowers lying on tabletops, hummingbirds and orchids in their natural settings, and salt marshes. Over four decades, Heade painted more than one hundred canvases depicting the salt marshes of the East Coast. This unusual landscape subject (virtually ignored by his contemporaries) was popular with his patrons, but Heade also was motivated by a continual desire to perfect his renderings. In his repetition of marsh scenes, albeit with minor compositional modifications, Heade could vary the effects of time of day, light, and weather—qualities that intrigued him throughout his career.

Heade traveled to many marshes in New England and New Jersey while he lived in New York during the 1860s and 1870s, then traded northeastern locales for the marshes he observed in Florida after his move there in 1883. The area north of Boston, including Marshfield, Newburyport, and Lynn, was one of his favorite destinations in the 1870s. In *Marshfield Meadows, Massachusetts*, the gentle, winding river leads the eye through the panoramic scene, while the placement of the hayricks gives it depth and scale. The rich green and brown palette, punctuated only by the red shirt of the tiny wagon driver, further reinforces the sense of tranquillity.

The painting's horizontality, its heavy atmosphere dominated by storm clouds, the contrasts of light and dark, and the minimal human presence are characteristics also found in Heade's *Thunderstorm Over Narragansett Bay* (see preceding plate). However, the earlier painting's romanticism and drama are here replaced by a sense of quietude, timelessness, and the enduring powers of nature.

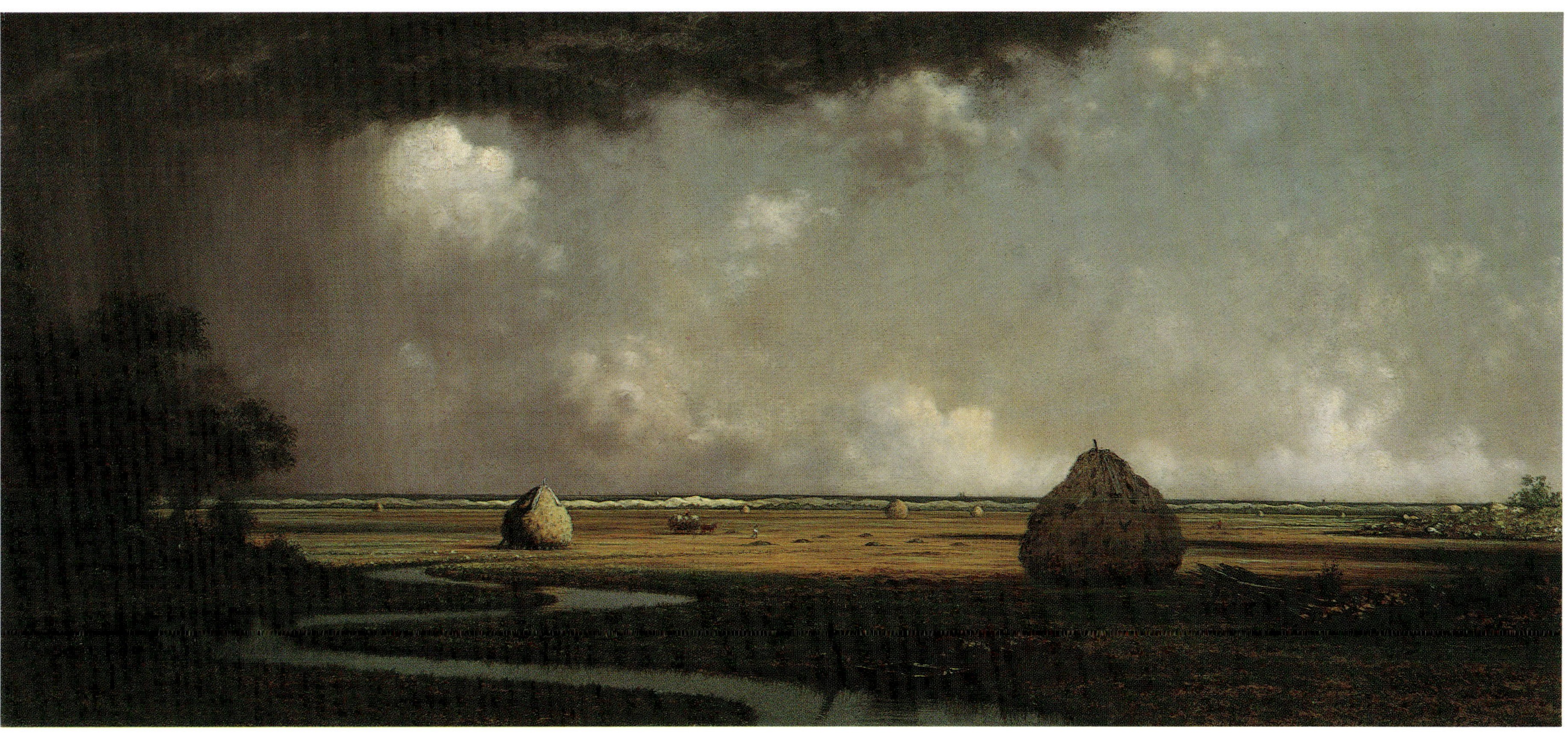

MARTIN JOHNSON HEADE
(1819–1904)

Two Hummingbirds Above a White Orchid

1870s
Oil on canvas, 18⅛ x 10⅛ in.
(46.0 x 25.7 cm)

Heade, encouraged by his friend Frederic Edwin Church, journeyed to South America three times in the 1860s. By the end of the decade, these trips had inspired him to begin painting his many canvases depicting hummingbirds in natural settings. *Two Hummingbirds Above a White Orchid* exemplifies Heade's development of this theme in his New York studio in the 1870s, when he typically incorporated one or more orchids (or occasionally passionflowers) into each scene. The controlled draughtsmanship and the bright palette of *Two Hummingbirds Above a White Orchid* complement the close-up, sharply focused view of the flower and attendant birds. In contrast to this specificity is the atmospheric rendering of a distant, lush South American setting, painted from memory. The painting beautifully expresses Heade's intense, lifelong study of nature in all its particularities.

Heade claimed to have been "almost a monomaniac" about hummingbirds since childhood. This may help to explain why, over the course of three or four decades, he produced at least fifty-four paintings of them. As early as 1863 or 1864, he studied Brazilian hummingbirds in a set of sixteen small paintings, and he began to include orchids in his compositions in 1871. The accuracy of detail about each species attests to the artist's close observation of his subjects during his South American travels.

By silhouetting orchids and hummingbirds against their native landscape, Heade created a new subject type in nineteenth-century American painting. These beautiful and highly inventive images defy classification as either still life or landscape, just as Heade's marsh scenes are neither landscape nor seascape, but instead literally where the two converge. His repeated treatment of these unusual subjects distinguishes Heade's paintings from the more conventional views painted by many of his contemporaries.

After marrying in 1883, Heade forsook his frequent travels and northeastern roots to settle in Saint Augustine, Florida. There he continued to paint marsh scenes and still lifes of cut flowers. While he did establish his first important relationship with a patron there and was the focal member of a small artists' colony, Heade died in obscurity, forgotten by the rest of the American art world.

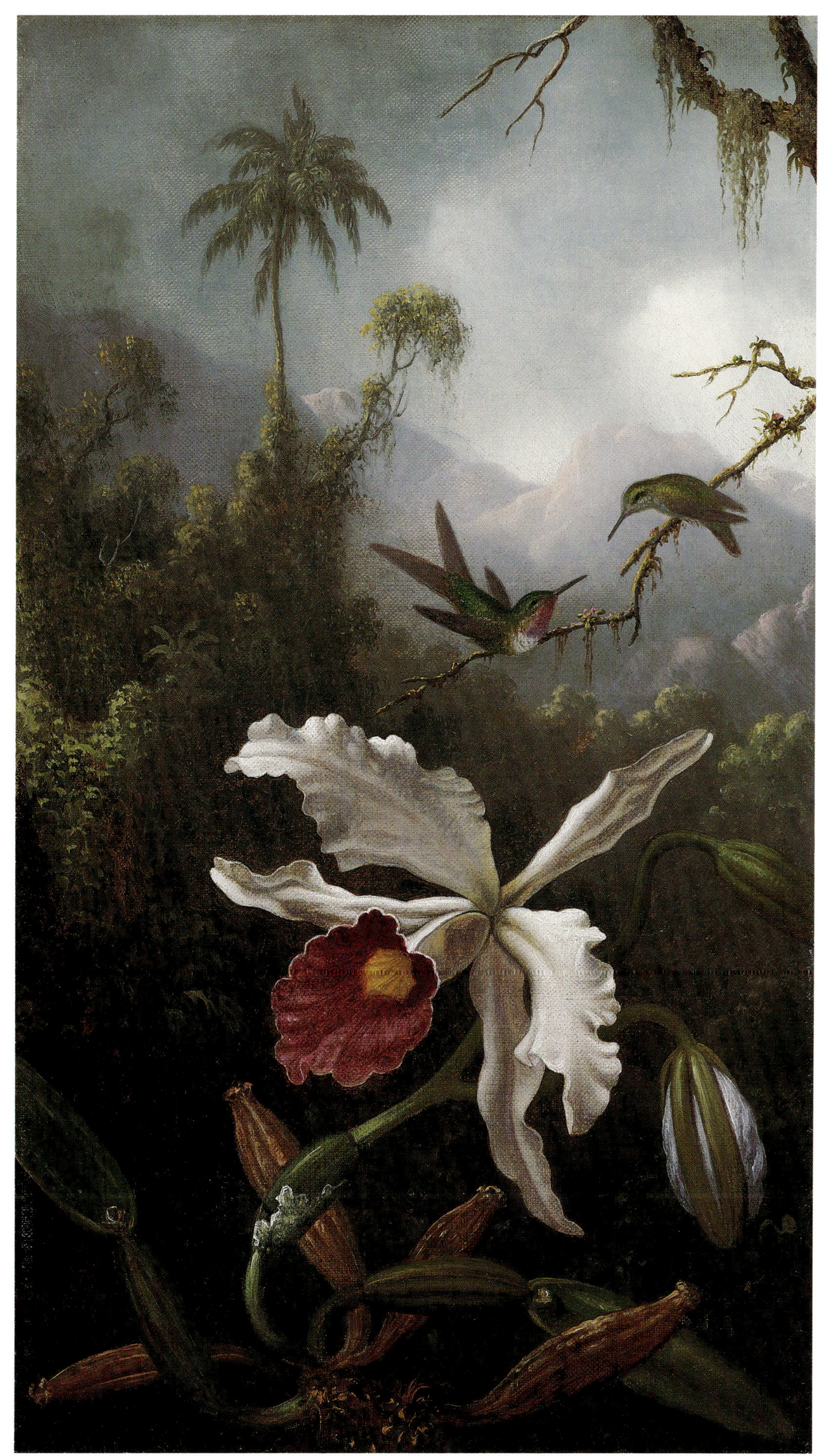

WORTHINGTON WHITTREDGE
(1820–1910)

On the Cache la Poudre River, Colorado

1876
Oil on canvas, 40⅜ x 60⅜ in.
(102.6 x 153.4 cm)

Worthington Whittredge, unlike other artist-explorers such as Thomas Moran and Albert Bierstadt, was interested in the serene, expansive plains of the West rather than its dramatic, rugged peaks and canyons. After painting in Cincinnati in the 1840s and studying in Europe in the 1850s, Whittredge achieved considerable critical recognition for his landscapes of eastern locations, which synthesized aspects of both Hudson River School and French Barbizon painting. Soon, however, he began to travel west in search of new, distinctly American subjects. *On the Cache la Poudre River, Colorado* was inspired by Whittredge's third and last trip to the West in 1871, when he also made studies of the Platte, Thompson, and St. Vrain Rivers.

In its technical mastery and great size, *On the Cache la Poudre River* represents the culmination of Whittredge's western landscapes. The delicately painted river view, depicting the valley area near Greeley, northeast of Denver, is populated only by the white-tailed deer grazing in the shade of towering cottonwood trees. The snow-capped Rockies, seen in the distance through a heavy haze, provide a striking contrast to the lush, inviting scene. The artist painted this large canvas in his New York studio five years after his return from Colorado, but he almost certainly based it on a small oil study (now in the Fine Arts Museums of San Francisco) that seems to have been executed on site.

Whittredge never again painted the western landscape but returned to the East for his later subject matter. His landscapes of New York State and New England depart from his earlier fusion of styles by increasingly reflecting Barbizon influences. The Museum's *A Breezy Day—Sakonnet Point, Rhode Island* (c. 1880) is a fine example of Whittredge's later work and displays affinities to the plein-air landscapes of French painters such as Charles-François Daubigny.

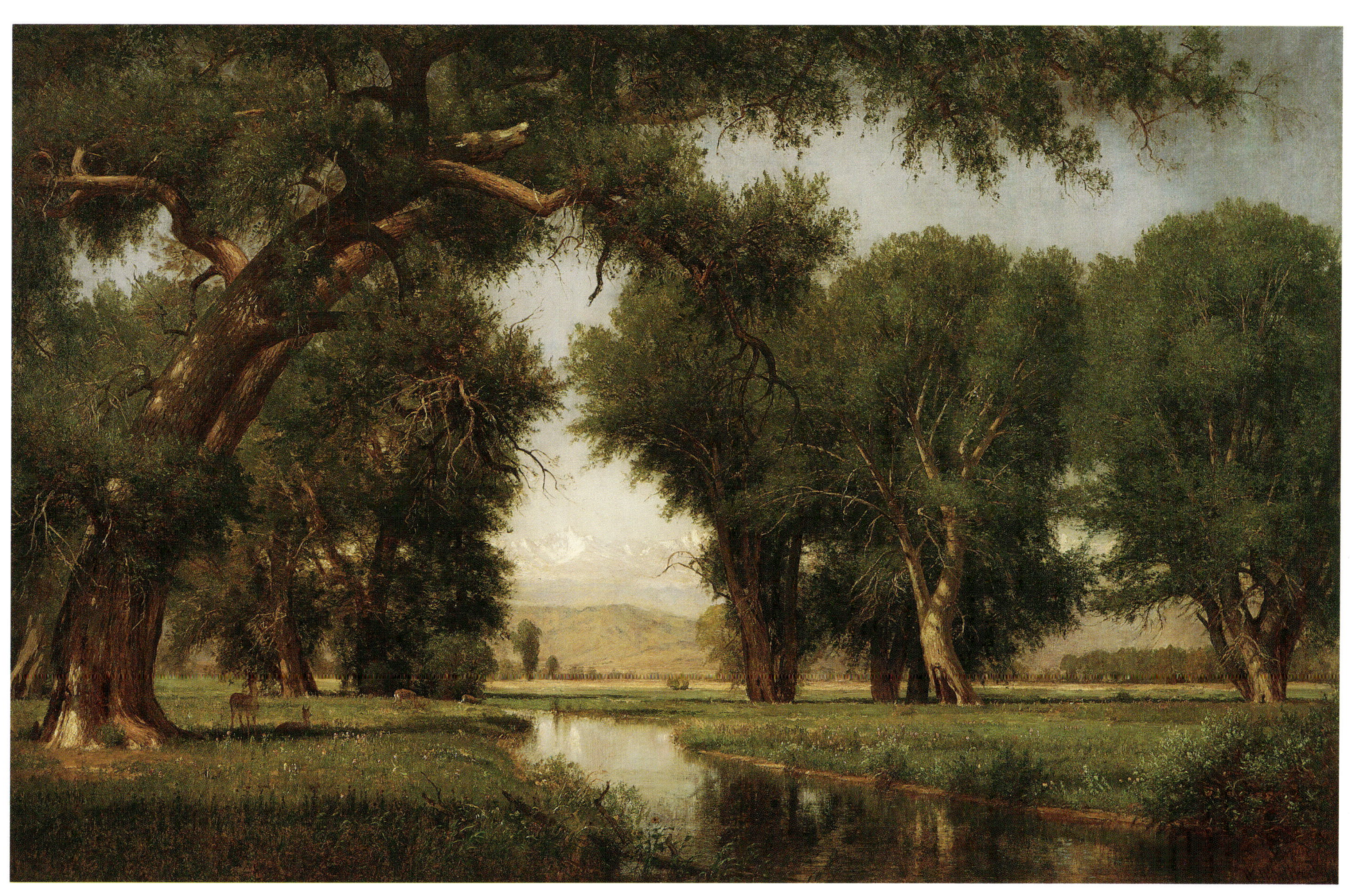

SEVERIN ROESEN

(1815 or 1816 – after 1872)

Still Life of Flowers and Fruit with a River Landscape in the Distance

1867
Oil on canvas, 35⅛ x 48⅛ in.
(89.2 x 123.2 cm)

Severin Roesen is today the best-known of all still-life painters who worked in America during the mid-nineteenth century. He introduced a totally new form of the genre into American art by reinterpreting traditional examples with greater bounty and occasional landscape details. His elaborate tabletop compositions, such as *Still Life of Flowers and Fruit with a River Landscape in the Distance*, rely on seventeenth- and eighteenth-century Dutch and German prototypes, which Roesen surely studied in his native Germany. The artist left Cologne in 1848, lived in New York for approximately ten years, then relocated to central Pennsylvania. He settled in the lumber town of Williamsport, where he achieved considerable local fame and success by painting large still lifes to adorn the dining rooms of the area's wealthy residents.

European influences abound in this painting's hard-edged clarity, bright palette, and sheer opulence of lush flowers and fruit set off by elegant glassware and the marble tabletop. Roesen's precise delineation of naturalistic details—water droplets on the flowers, feathers in the bird's nest, the lemon's refraction in the goblet, and the vase's translucency—also derives from the northern European still-life tradition. To render the nineteenth-century theme of America's natural abundance, Roesen united still life with a landscape background, featuring a wooded grove at the left and a mountainous river scene at the right (probably the nearby Susquehanna River and Allegheny Mountains). This union of two genres would also appear a decade later in Martin Johnson Heade's *Two Hummingbirds Above a White Orchid* (see plate on page 27). However, where Heade concentrated on individual examples of flora and fauna in their natural settings, Roesen portrayed a profusion of formally arranged fruits and flowers.

Roesen painted hundreds of still lifes in his lifetime and died sometime after 1872, the year of his last dated work. He often repeated compositional groupings in his canvases, suggesting that he used stencils or copied certain motifs, either from his own studies or from prints of works by other artists—practices not uncommon in the nineteenth century. Thus, despite their naturalistic appearances, his still lifes often combine species of flowers and fruits from different growing seasons. Artistic prerogative aside, Roesen's still lifes are among the most beautiful produced in America during the nineteenth century, and, in their exquisite detail, they continually invite the viewer's closer inspection.

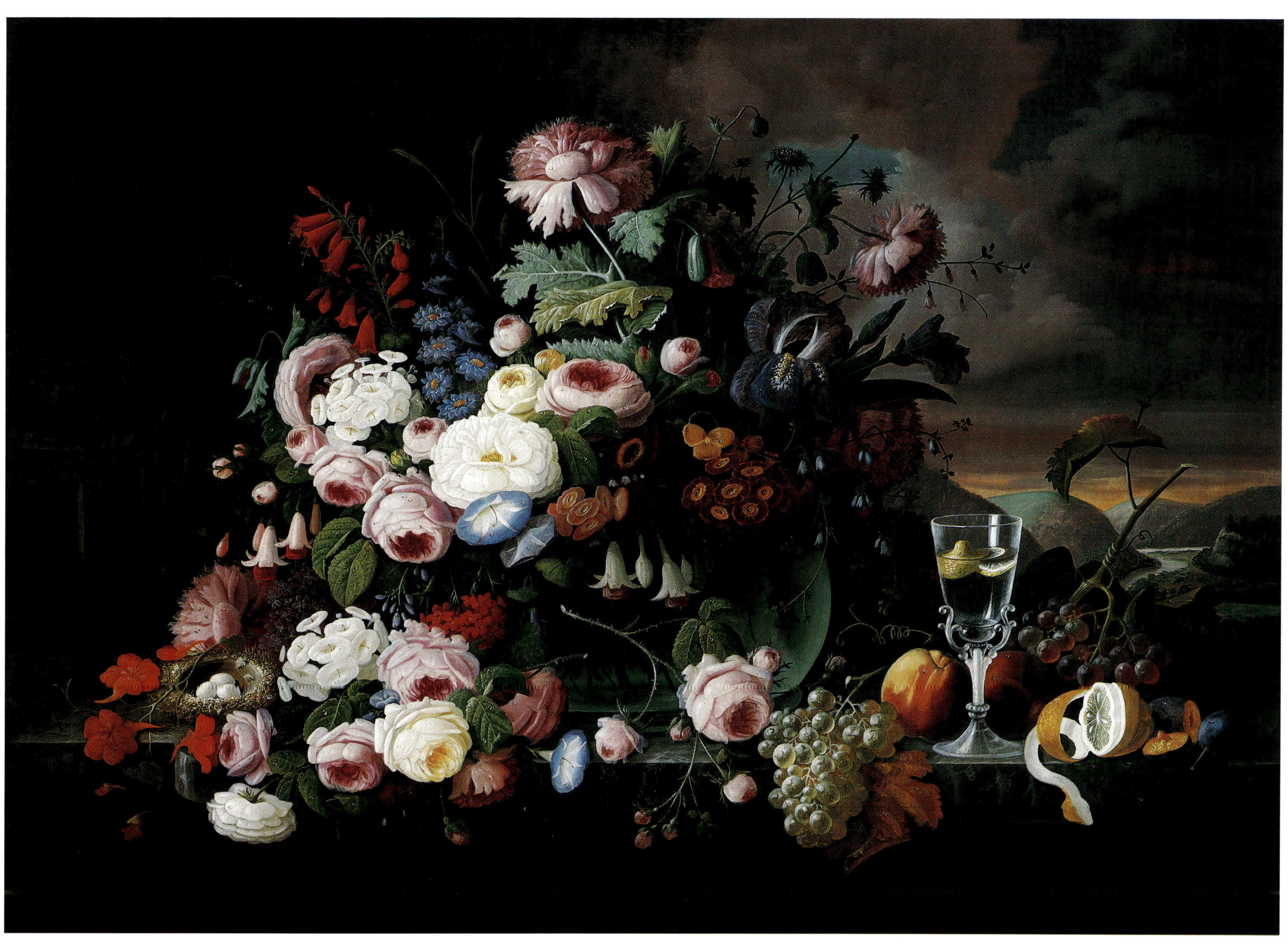

WILLIAM MICHAEL HARNETT

(1848–1892)

Ease

1887
Oil on canvas, 48 x 52¾ in.
(121.9 x 134 cm)

William M. Harnett was the leading painter of trompe-l'oeil (literally "fool-the-eye") still lifes in late nineteenth-century America. Unlike the highly personal letter rack paintings of John F. Peto or the elegant fruit pieces of William McCloskey, Harnett's unique still lifes effectively function as composite portraits of the wealthy middle-class patrons who commissioned them. In the hard-edged, highly illusionistic style that was his signature, Harnett rendered groups of objects that alluded to the occupations and leisurely pursuits of businessmen and merchants.

The Irish-born artist spent his youth in Philadelphia; in the 1860s and 1870s he attended art academies there and in New York City while working as a silver engraver. In 1880, he went abroad for six years to paint and study the seventeenth-century European still-life masters (primarily in Munich), then returned to New York in 1886 to begin his most productive period.

Harnett's largest tabletop still life, *Ease*, was commissioned by wealthy Massachusetts businessman James T. Abbe, owner of the Holyoke Envelope Company and president of the company that published the *Springfield Daily Union*. Envelopes postmarked Holyoke and a newspaper attest to Abbe's professional ventures, while books such as William Cullen Bryant's *Popular History of the United States* and an account book with references to Harriet Beecher Stowe's *Uncle Tom's Cabin* suggest his literary and political interests. The metal cup, ewer, and richly patterned table covering signify his prominent social standing. Although the violin, flute, and sheet music are symbolic of Abbe's cultural refinement, Harnett used such objects in many other "bric-a-brac" paintings. The smoldering cigar, suggesting Abbe's recent departure, lends a personal yet haunting touch to the composition.

Although Harnett had executed other tabletop still lifes earlier in his career, *Ease* reflects his absorption of the dark palette, strong gradations of light and shade, and elaborate compositions of the Old Master paintings he studied while in Europe. Harnett's highly tactile rendering of textures and luminous surfaces and his carefully arranged pyramidal composition further the sense of opulence. In this grand deception, the objects seem solid, as if occupying three-dimensional space, and some, such as the newspaper and sheet music, even appear to project out of the picture plane toward the viewer.

When Harnett died at the age of forty-four, five years after completing *Ease*, his productivity had been diminished for several years by severe arthritis. His considerable reputation subsequently fell into decline, and rediscovery of his works began only in 1935. *Ease* itself was thought destroyed and was known only through a contemporary photograph and newspaper account until it reappeared in 1971. In addition to *Ease*, the Museum owns *Attention, Company!*, one of Harnett's rare figural works.

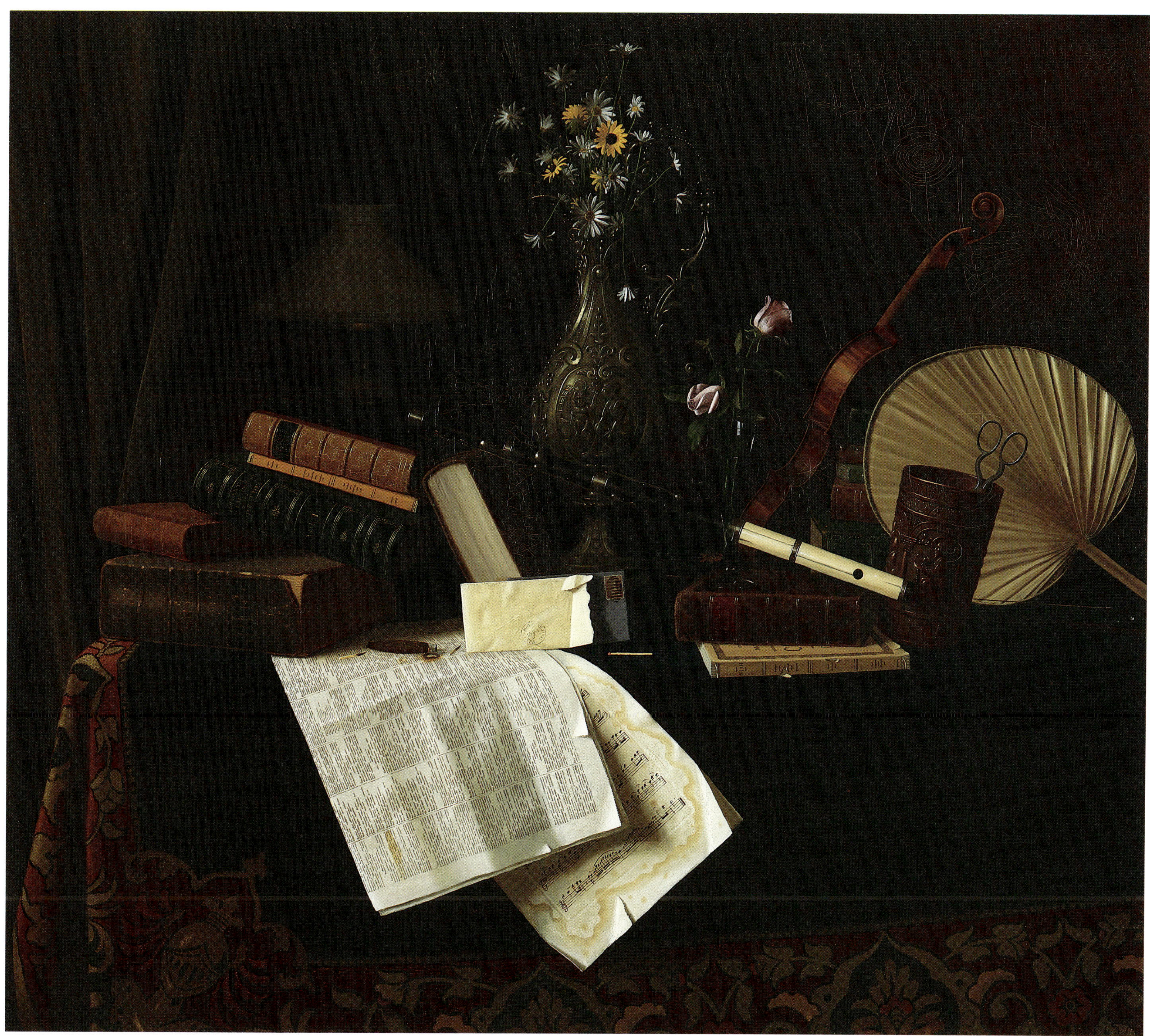

WILLIAM J. McCLOSKEY
(1859–1941)

Wrapped Oranges

1889
Oil on canvas, 12 x 16 in.
(30.5 x 40.6 cm)
Acquisition in memory of Katrine Deakins, Trustee, Amon Carter Museum, 1961–1985

William McCloskey's simple yet exquisitely painted still lifes have been rediscovered only in recent years, making the artist one of an increasing number of nineteenth-century painters whose reputations are undergoing revival.

Due to his peripatetic nature, little is known of the artist's life. In the late 1870s, he studied at the Pennsylvania Academy of the Fine Arts under such influential teachers as Thomas Eakins. According to the inscriptions on *Wrapped Oranges* and another painting of the same subject (private collection), he was in New York in 1889 and 1901. He also lived and painted in various locales in the West and in Europe and died in California, where he worked as a portrait painter for the last twenty years of his life.

McCloskey seems to have been aware of the great still lifes produced earlier in the nineteenth century by members of Philadelphia's Peale family—especially the restrained, elegant tabletop fruit paintings of Raphaelle Peale. The exacting realism of *Wrapped Oranges* may also reflect some familiarity with William M. Harnett's trompe-l'oeil still lifes, which were well known in Philadelphia in the late 1870s and in New York in the 1880s.

Wrapped Oranges is an unusual treatment of the European-influenced, highly realistic style of still-life painting practiced in late-nineteenth-century America. His contemporaries—including Harnett, John F. Peto, and John Haberle—favored complex arrangements of man-made objects, but McCloskey chose a simple composition of brilliant oranges wrapped in crisp tissue paper. To complete this magnificent illusion, the tabletop reflects the radiant wrapped fruit, and the rich Prussian blue background complements the arrangement. The delicately rendered tissue paper in *Wrapped Oranges* was McCloskey's trademark; he also included it in his other still lifes of wrapped lemons and of berries spilling out of baskets.

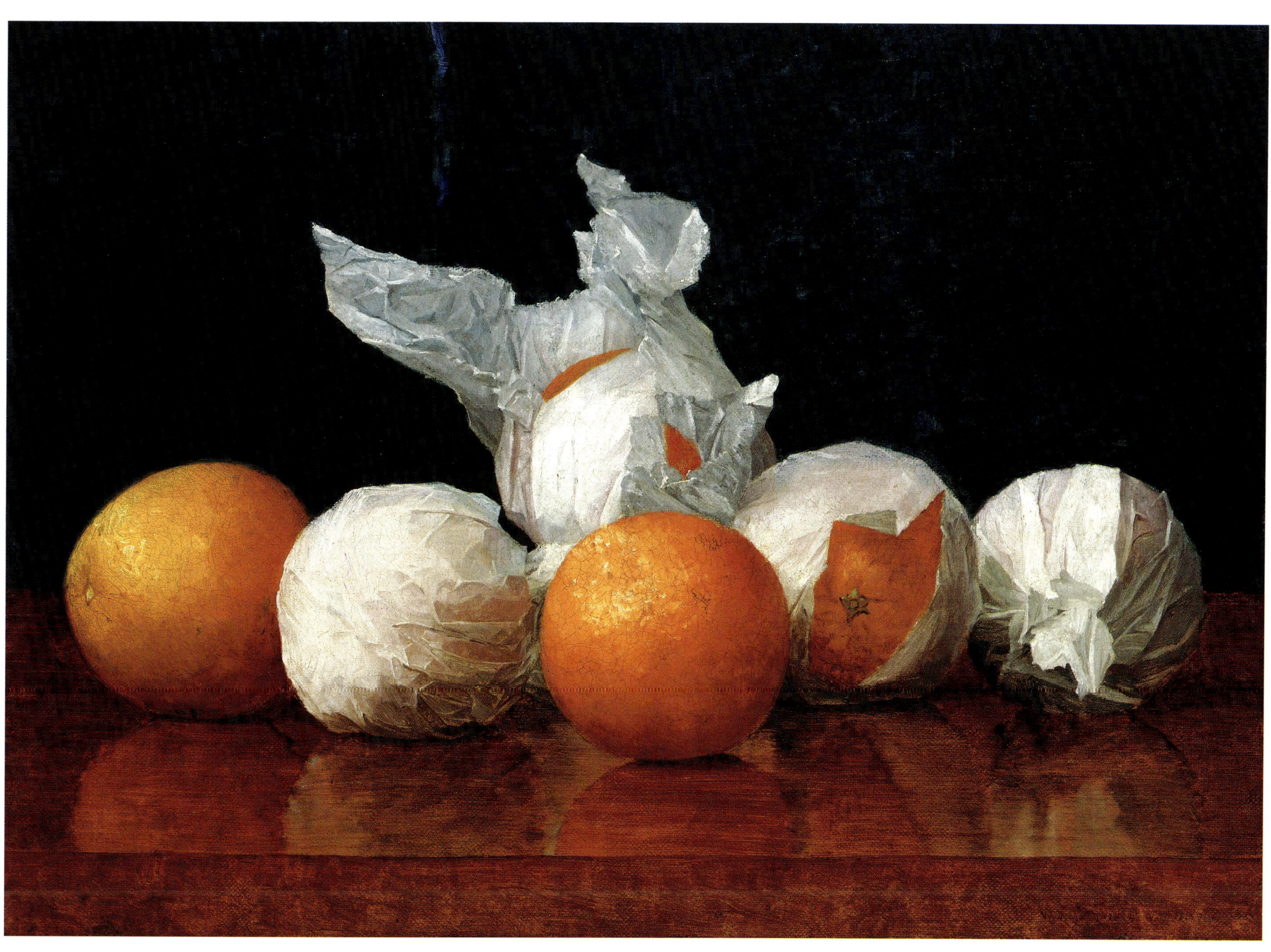

JOHN FREDERICK PETO
(1854–1907)

A Closet Door

1904/1906
Oil on canvas, 40¼ x 30⅛ in.
(102.2 x 76.5 cm)

John Frederick Peto and his friend William Harnett were the leading exponents of trompe-l'oeil still-life painting in late nineteenth-century America and the only major American practitioners of a European-derived genre, the letter rack picture. *A Closet Door* is a masterful example of this subject type, in which letters and other objects appear to be secured to wooden panels by stretched tapes. Peto began painting these works around 1879, first on speculation or commission as trade signs and, later, for friends and neighbors.

Peto studied briefly at the Pennsylvania Academy of the Fine Arts and spent the 1880s painting in his native Philadelphia. He was greatly influenced by Harnett's work but remained somewhat withdrawn from the Philadelphia artistic mainstream and exhibited only a few works at the Academy. Married in 1887, Peto settled in 1889 in Island Heights, New Jersey, where he focused his energies on family life and community activities as well as on painting letter racks and tabletop still lifes.

A Closet Door, Peto's last known letter rack painting, reflects the artist's increasingly personal and introspective style in this genre, as well as his mastery of design and illusionistic rendering. In it, he combines everyday items such as an almanac and a Victorian book with objects of more enigmatic significance, including a portrait of George Washington and assorted letters and cards. Some of these articles may have autobiographical significance, such as the self-addressed letter postmarked "Philadelphia"; Peto's other letter rack pictures commonly contain such personal references.

Peto's works symbolically suggest the passage of time by incorporating well-worn objects, such as the rusting horseshoe, nails, key, broken hinges, frayed ribbon, and torn and folded papers of *A Closet Door*. Old, dilapidated articles are also the subject of his tabletop still lifes, such as the Museum's *Lamps of Other Days* (c. 1900). Like his choice of subjects, Peto's soft-edged technique and often muted palette distinguish his paintings from the works of Harnett, whose crystalline treatment of more elegant, opulent items is exemplified in the Museum's painting, *Ease* (see plate on page 33). Nevertheless, from the rediscovery of Harnett in the 1930s until that of Peto in the next decade, many Peto paintings were thought to have been painted by Harnett in a second, "softer" style, and some were even given false signatures.

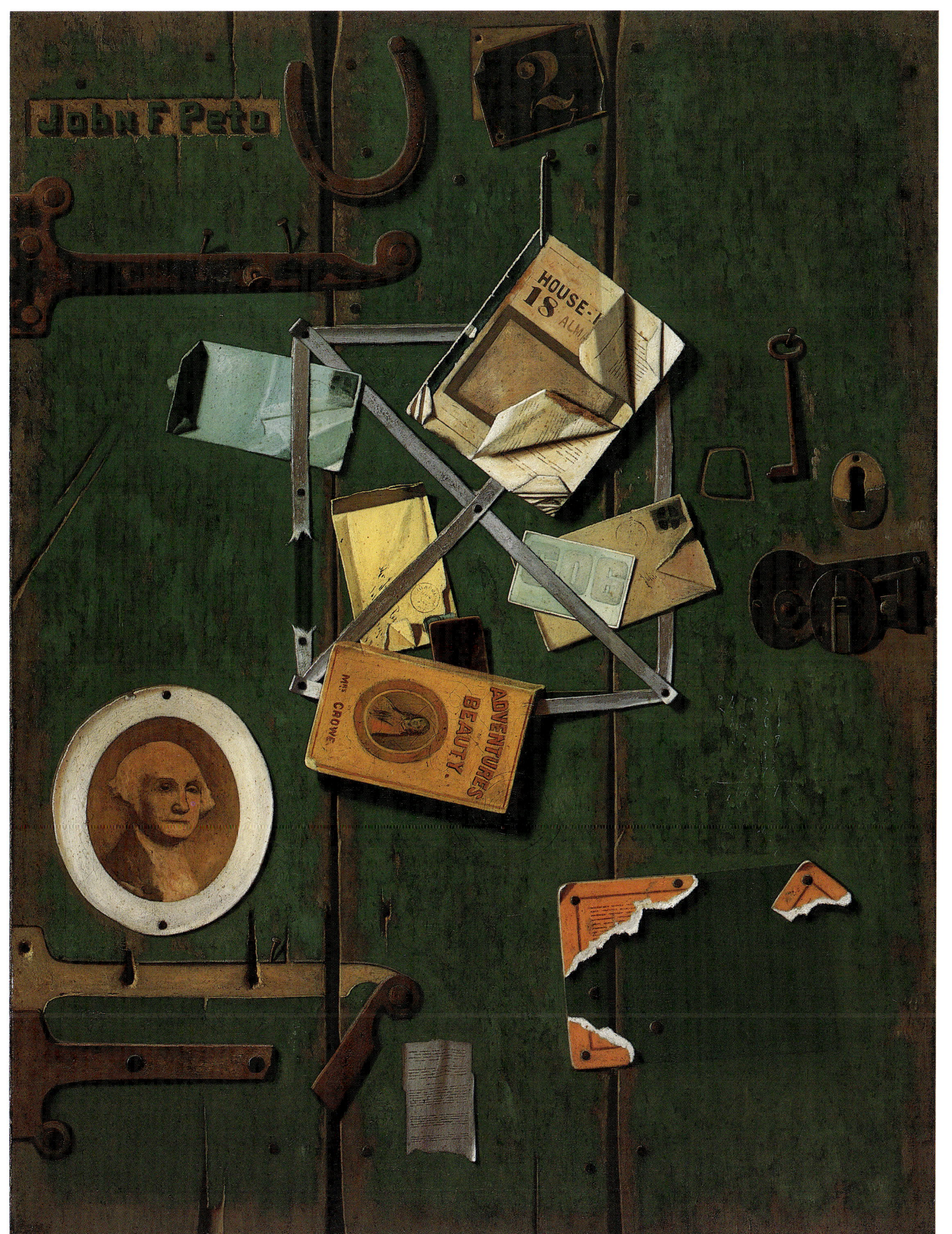

John F Peto
2
HOUSE-
18
ADVENTURES
BEAUTY.
Mrs CROWE

WINSLOW HOMER
(1836–1910)

Crossing the Pasture

c. 1872
Oil on canvas, 26¼ x 38⅛ in.
(66.7 x 96.8 cm)

Winslow Homer trained as a lithographer in Boston and worked until the late 1870s as a free-lance illustrator, covering the Civil War and other subjects for such magazines as *Harper's Weekly*. He took up painting in about 1861, two years after he moved to New York, and spent each spring, summer, and fall of the next twenty years sketching in the northeastern countryside. Like many nineteenth-century landscapists, in the winters Homer returned to his New York studio to paint his canvases.

Crossing the Pasture exemplifies Homer's work of the early 1870s, when he made oil paintings and watercolors of farm children in the Catskill Mountains. Unlike the sentimental representations of children by his contemporaries, the boys in Homer's painting have solemn expressions that mitigate the pastoral scene around them. A sense of foreboding is suggested by the larger child's protective stance and shouldered switch. A bull, either the one in the left background or one out of view, may be the perceived threat of danger. As in many of Homer's works, however, the painting's somewhat unsettling tone is balanced by its painterly beauty and careful design. The two figures, linked by the glistening pail, occupy the center of the composition, and the larger boy's head marks almost exactly the crossing of the two slopes behind them. The bull at the left is balanced compositionally by the house and another bull at the lower end of the meadow, and the whole is unified by the dabs of bright pigment that define the wildflowers and highlight the bull, trees, rocks, and house.

Homer traveled extensively in search of subject matter. During a pivotal trip to the coast of England in 1881–82, he completed the Museum's drawing *Blyth Sands* (1882). Upon his return to the United States, he settled in Prout's Neck, Maine, and began producing many paintings, watercolors, and drawings of the area's rugged coast and its hardy fishermen and villagers. From Maine, he continued to travel—visiting Quebec and the Adirondacks in the summers and the Bahamas, Bermuda, and Florida during the winter—and painted brilliant watercolors that have earned him credit as one of America's finest practitioners in that medium.

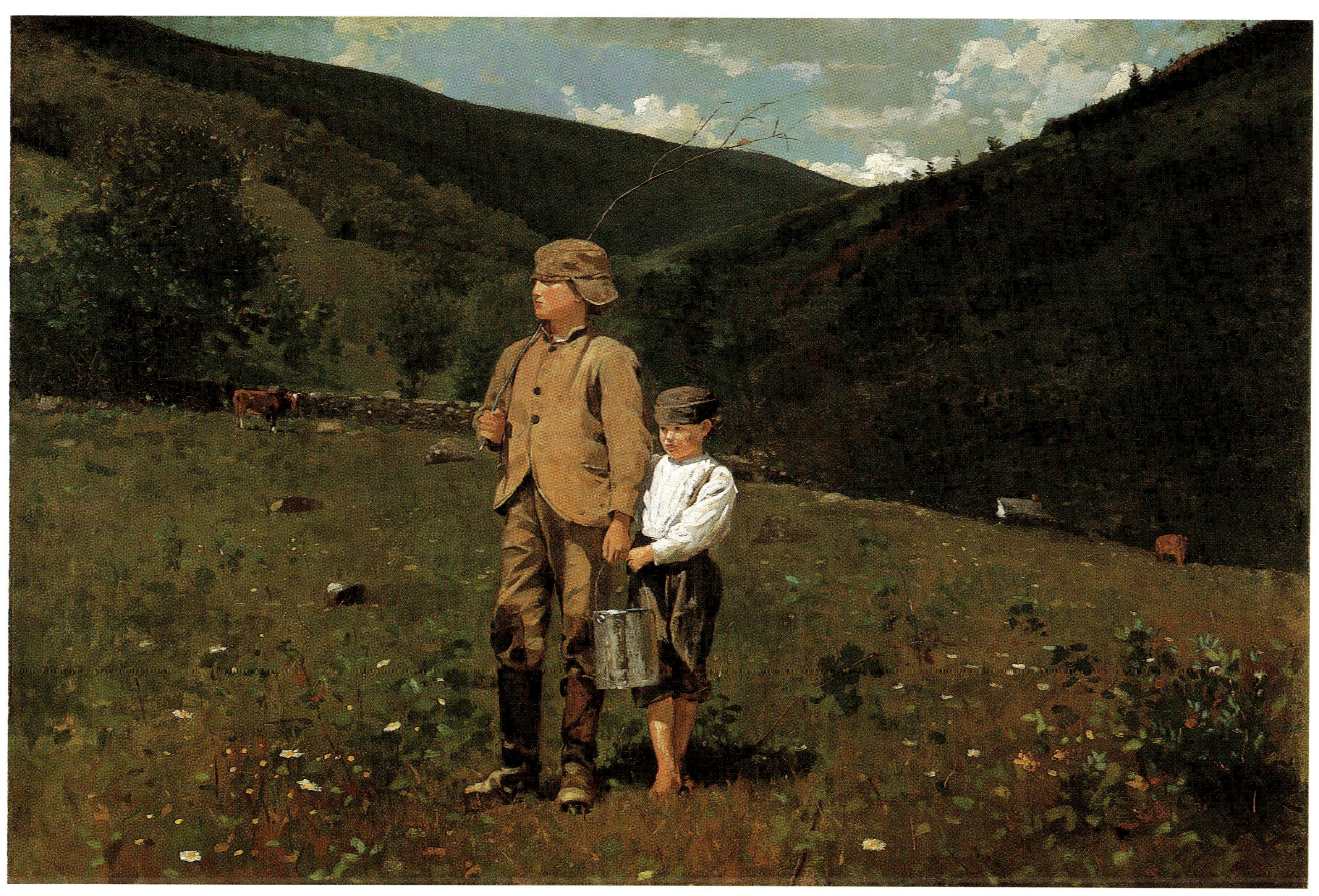

THOMAS EAKINS
(1844–1916)

The Swimming Hole

c. 1883–85
Oil on canvas, 27 5/16 x 36 5/16 in.
(69.4 x 92.2 cm)
Purchased by the Friends of Art, Fort Worth Art Association, 1925; acquired by the Amon Carter Museum, 1990, from the Modern Art Museum of Fort Worth through grants and donations from the Amon G. Carter Foundation, the Sid W. Richardson Foundation, the Anne Burnett and Charles Tandy Foundation, Capital Cities/ABC Foundation, *Fort Worth Star-Telegram*, the R. D. and Joan Dale Hubbard Foundation, and the people of Fort Worth.

Thomas Eakins was one of the most influential yet controversial painters and teachers in nineteenth-century America. His incisive realism at times caused his patrons to reject their completed portraits, and his belief that students should study the human figure from live models rather than plaster casts was a major factor in his dismissal from a teaching post at the Pennsylvania Academy of the Fine Arts.

Throughout his career, Eakins was interested in the precise, realistic depiction of human anatomy and movement. The Philadelphia native studied art and anatomy at the Academy beginning in 1862 and undertook further anatomy study at Jefferson Medical College. Between 1866 and 1870, he traveled in Europe and studied with the French master Jean-Léon Gérôme. He then took more anatomy classes in Philadelphia and assumed teaching posts at the Philadelphia Sketch Club and at the Pennsylvania Academy. About 1880, while continuing to paint, Eakins began to experiment with photography, taking as his primary subject the human figure in motion.

Eakins' extensive study of the human form is evident in his masterpiece, *The Swimming Hole*. Painted during his teaching years at the Pennsylvania Academy, the work depicts Eakins himself in the water at the lower right, with his setter Harry, and some of his students and friends relaxing and swimming at the edge of a shady riverbank near Philadelphia. The poses and gestures which link the figures around the rocky outcropping and the resulting pyramidal grouping are classical in feeling, reflecting Eakins' study of the Academy's plaster casts of antique sculpture. Eakins also carefully chose each figure's pose so that the group collectively represents a complete cycle of motion, from the swimming Eakins to the climbing, resting, standing, and finally diving figures. Working from oil sketches, photographs of the students and surrounding landscape, and at least one wax model of one of the figures, Eakins created a delicately composed yet seemingly casual scene of the timeless enjoyment of nature. Like his well-known portraits, *The Swimming Hole* unites classical inspiration with an unmistakably modern approach.

The Swimming Hole was included in the annual exhibition of the Pennsylvania Academy of the Fine Arts in 1885, about two years after Eakins set to work on it. Soon after his expulsion from the Academy in 1886, the artist and some of his students established the Philadelphia Art Students League. Eakins was only moderately well-known outside Philadelphia during his lifetime and was frequently criticized there; only toward the end of his life did he receive any significant recognition in the art world. However, his relentless championing of the unsentimental portrayal of contemporary subjects set an important precedent for later American realists.

In spite of its modest presentation of figures in an idyllic setting, the patron who commissioned *The Swimming Hole* exchanged it for one of Eakins' portraits. In 1925, the Modern Art Museum of Fort Worth, then known as the Fort Worth Art Association, purchased the painting from Eakins' widow. It was acquired by the Amon Carter Museum in 1990, thereby ensuring the work's continued enjoyment by the people of Fort Worth.

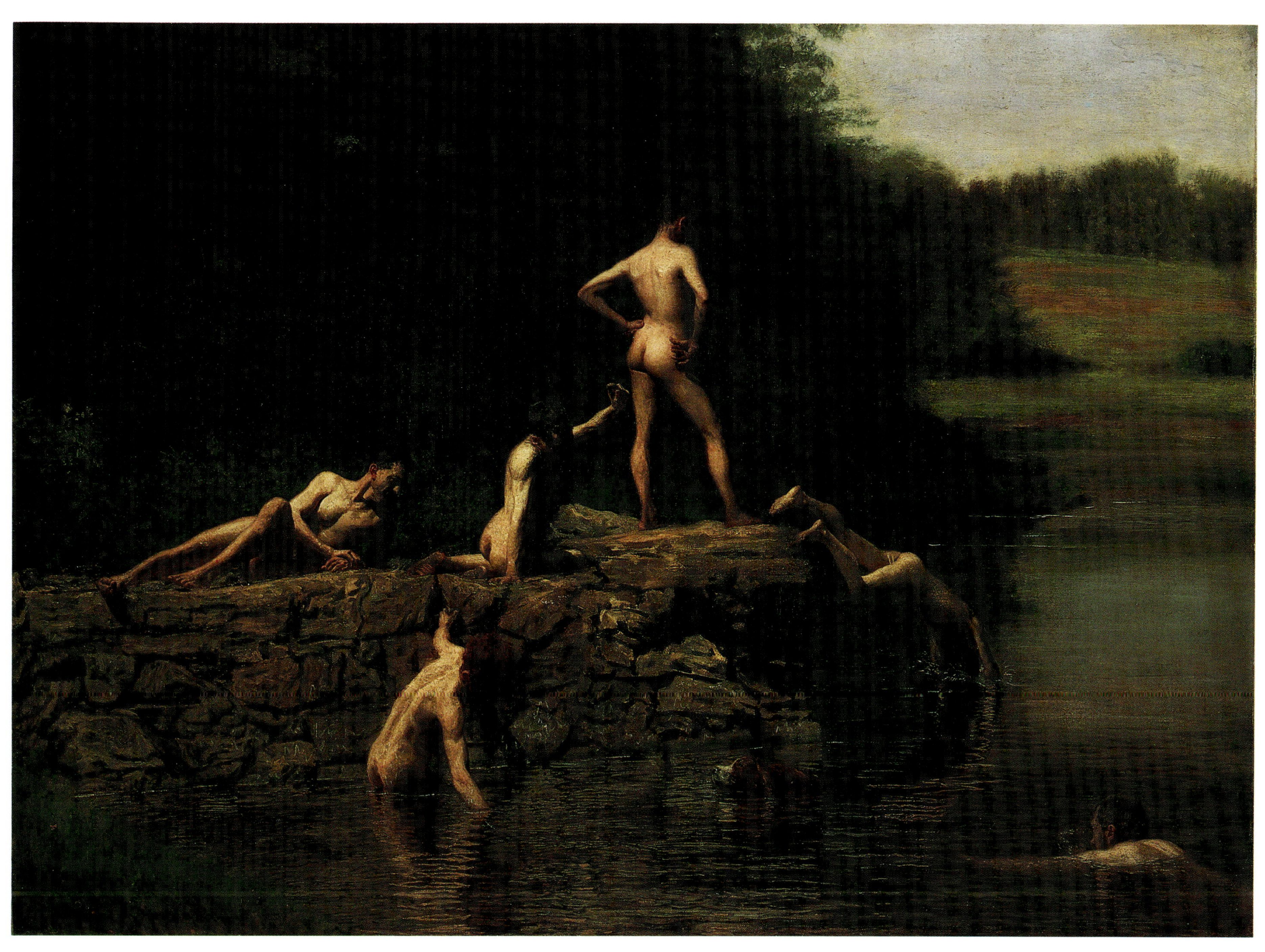

WILLIAM MERRITT CHASE
(1849–1916)

Idle Hours

c. 1894
Oil on canvas, 25½ x 35½ in.
(64.8 x 90.2 cm)

A successful artist, influential teacher, and relentless champion of American art, William Merritt Chase was one of the most highly regarded figures of the late-nineteenth-century American art world. He received his artistic training primarily at the Royal Academy in Munich, and upon his return from Europe to New York City in 1878, he assumed leading roles in arts organizations, taught at the Art Students League, and exhibited his work frequently. Beginning in 1891, the artist left New York City each summer for the open spaces and bright light of Shinnecock Hills, Long Island, where he founded America's largest and most respected school for open-air painting.

During this period Chase produced a group of idyllic, light-filled paintings of his family at the seaside, including *Idle Hours*. The painting shows his wife, reading in the sun, his two daughters, and a third figure who may be his sister-in-law. The Shinnecock views mark a radical departure from Chase's earlier works and are some of the finest achievements of his career. The dramatic shift in the artist's surroundings only partly accounts for his new subject of outdoor leisure, his brightened palette, and an interest in the changing effects of light on the landscape. These works also show the influence of French impressionism, with its emphasis on recording fleeting moments by painting in the open air.

The expansive sky and brilliant light, the delicately rendered layers of clouds (some of which portend a rising storm), and the languid poses of the figures in *Idle Hours* exemplify Chase's unrivalled ability to evoke a mood and a sense of place in his shore scenes. The composition's graceful curves and the muted but rich palette, punctuated by small notes of red, reinforce the painting's peaceful tone. Chase's virtuoso brushwork furthers the sense of freshness and immediacy. It is no artistic illusion that *Idle Hours* appears to have been painted rapidly; at Shinnecock, Chase sometimes completed as many as two canvases within a week.

Chase closed the Shinnecock Summer School of Art in 1902 but continued to teach at various New York and Philadelphia art schools until 1911. In 1905 he joined the group of American impressionist painters known as "The Ten" and taught summer art classes in Europe from 1903 until shortly before his death.

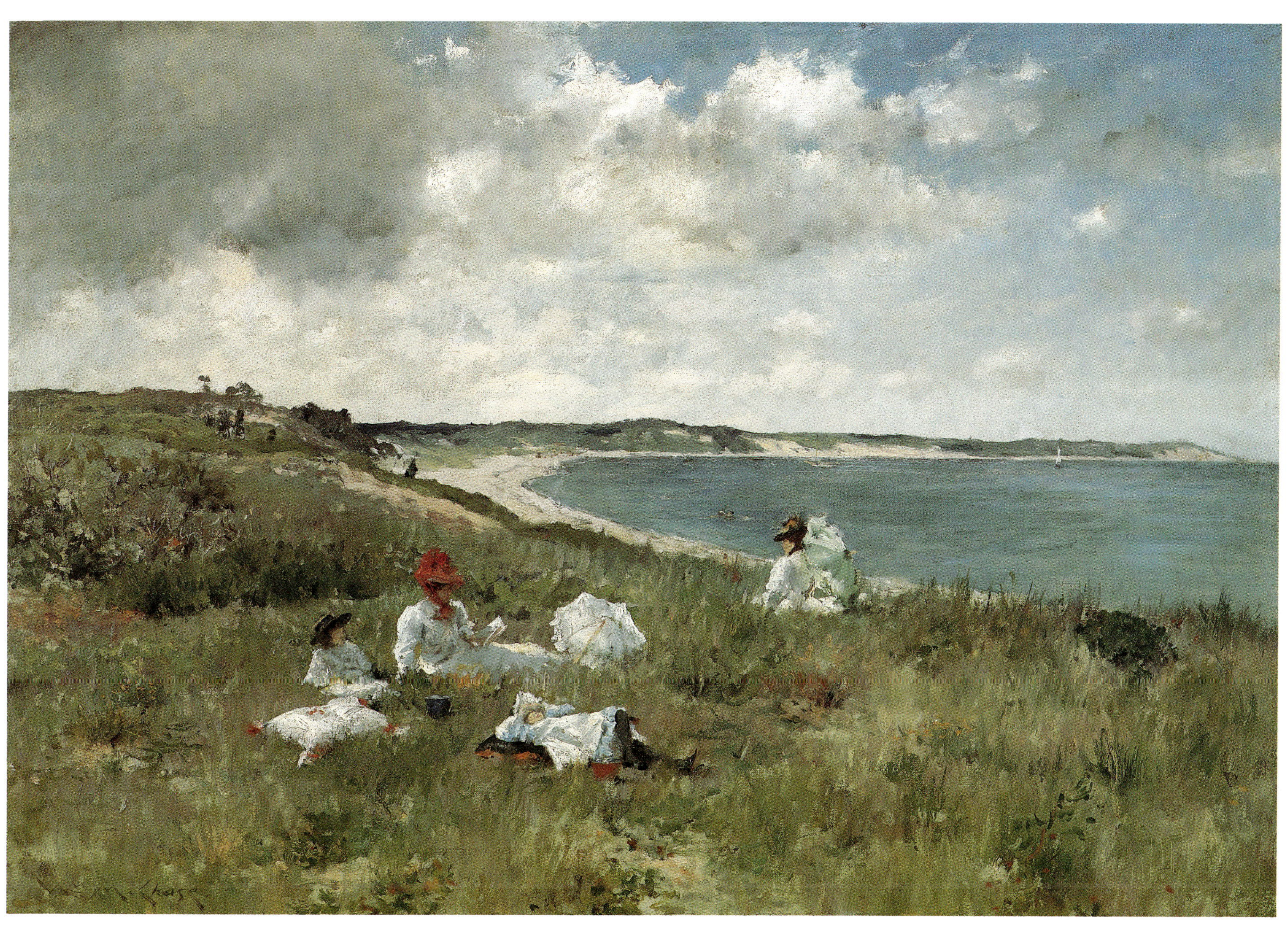

MARY CASSATT
(1844–1926)

Mother and Daughter, Both Wearing Large Hats (Fillette au grand chapeau)

1900–01
Oil on canvas, 32 x 26 in.
(81.3 x 66 cm)
Gift of Ruth Carter Stevenson in honor of Adelyn Dohme Breeskin, Trustee, Amon Carter Museum, 1972–1982

Mary Cassatt was one of the few women and the only American painter accepted into the circle of the French impressionists in the late nineteenth century. After training at the Pennsylvania Academy of the Fine Arts in the 1860s, she undertook less formal study while traveling in Europe. In 1877, three years after settling permanently in Paris, the artist was invited to join the impressionists; she subsequently participated in their controversial exhibitions. Around 1890 Cassatt began frequent treatments of her best-known theme, maternity, which is beautifully represented in *Mother and Daughter, Both Wearing Large Hats*.

The painting's garden setting suggests that it was executed at Chateau Beaufresne, Cassatt's country house outside Paris. The models, though unidentified, were possibly a mother and daughter who lived nearby. Wearing the fashionable dresses and hats that Cassatt loved and often provided to her models for sittings, the woman and child are depicted in an intimate yet unsentimental relationship. While Cassatt unites the two figures through the repetition of circles—in their arms, faces, and hats—and with a pink-toned lap covering that they share, their solemn expressions and independent gazes suggest distinct identities. This duality of character differentiates Cassatt's images of maternity from her contemporaries' often overtly sentimental portrayals of women and children engaged in quiet domestic activity. In style, her loose brushstroke and light palette reflect the influence of her French associates. Like her close friend and mentor Degas, Cassatt is distinguished from the other impressionists by her strong sense of draughtsmanship and compositional design, as well as her use of black, so richly employed in the ribbon on the child's oversized hat.

Cassatt's friendship with Edgar Degas was significant in several ways for the careers of both artists. He inspired her to take up printmaking and pastel, media in which she excelled, and introduced her to the Japanese influences that she frequently drew upon in her prints and paintings. Cassatt also advised several respected American collectors in their first purchases of French impressionist painting, and she was especially successful in promoting the work of Degas. Although increasing illness forced her to give up her art around 1910, she remained in her beloved Paris until her death.

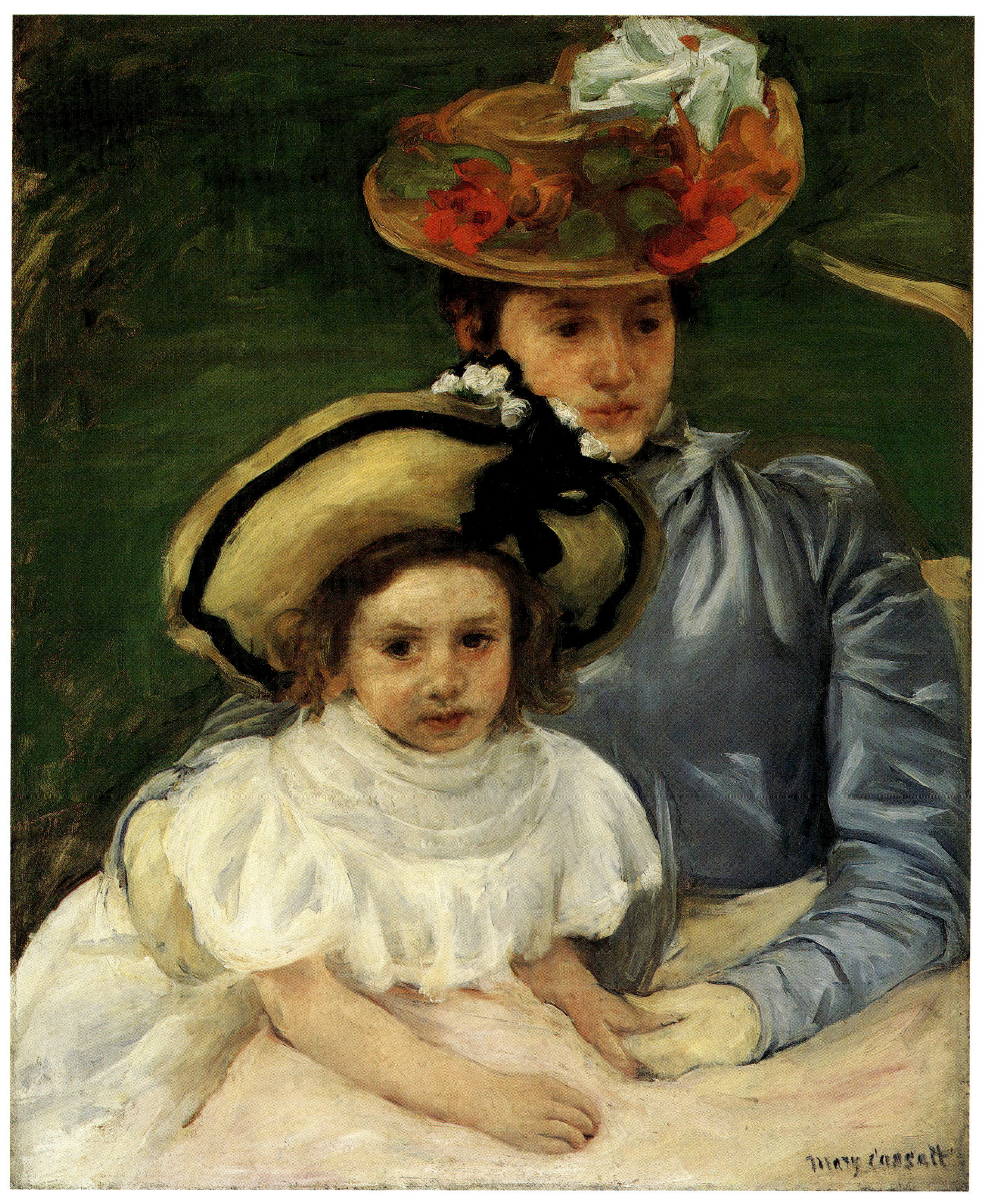
Mary Cassatt

ARTHUR G. DOVE
(1880–1946)

The Lobster

1908
Oil on canvas, 25⅞ x 32 in.
(65.7 x 81.3 cm)
Acquisition in memory of Anne Burnett Tandy, Trustee, Amon Carter Museum, 1968–1980

Arthur G. Dove was one of a pioneering group of artists whose increasingly abstract style, developed under the influence of European modernism, radically changed the course of American art. After graduating from Cornell University, Dove worked as a magazine illustrator for five years in New York City, then moved to Paris in 1908 to study art. There the American artists Alfred Maurer and Arthur B. Carles encouraged him to study the works of the impressionists and fauves. During this pivotal period the artist painted *The Lobster*, with its fluid brushwork, heavy black outlines, vivid palette, and patterned abstraction reflecting the influence of Paul Cézanne and Henri Matisse. The curvilinear rhythms of flowers and vines in the background relate directly to decorative motifs found in Matisse's work, while the structured composition, fragmented planes, and coarse modeling are indebted to the still lifes of Cézanne.

Dove painted landscapes in the French countryside yet must have considered *The Lobster* the best example of his work of this period, for on his return to New York he left the painting in Paris to be exhibited in the 1909 Autumn Salon. The canvas was to gain further importance for Dove's career when it became one of the first works he showed to Alfred Stieglitz, the highly influential New York gallery owner and promoter of modern art. Included in Stieglitz' important 1910 exhibition "Younger American Painters," *The Lobster* shocked the New York art world with its sinuous rhythms and flat patterning of vibrant colors and shapes.

The exhibition marked the beginning of Stieglitz' lifelong encouragement of Dove through frequent exhibition opportunities, financial assistance, and friendship; these helped to ease Dove's struggle to survive in the conservative art world of the early twentieth century. (Other American modernists who enjoyed Stieglitz' unfailing support included Georgia O'Keeffe, John Marin, Marsden Hartley, and Charles Demuth, whose works are also represented in the Museum's collection.) In spite of such promotion, however, Dove never found consistent acceptance or patronage for his often experimental and abstract works; even Stieglitz once noted that some of the artist's works were "above the heads of the people." Nevertheless, Dove vigorously pursued his art and continued to develop his own unique style well beyond his early European experiments.

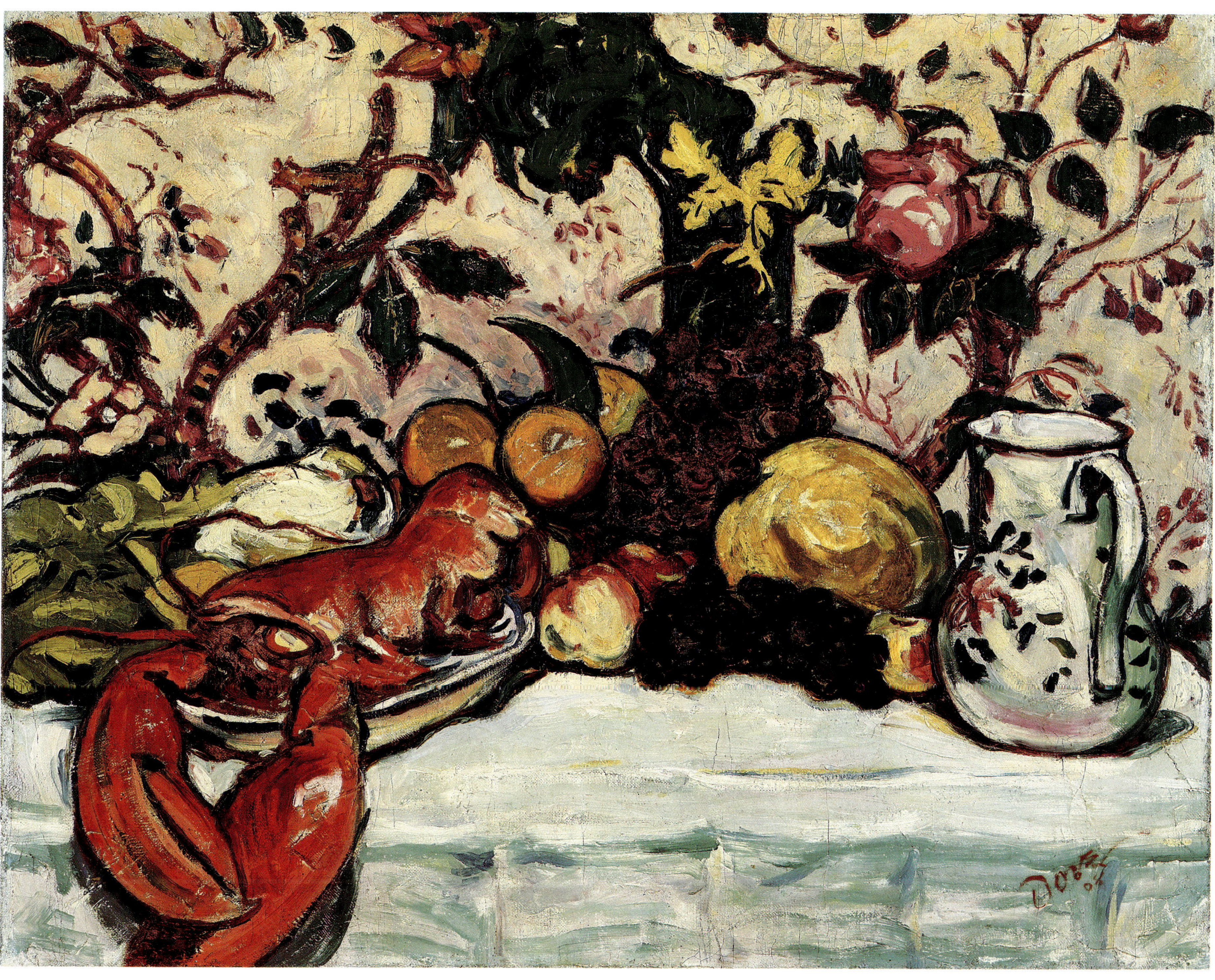

ARTHUR G. DOVE
(1880–1946)

Thunder Shower

1940
Oil and wax emulsion on canvas, 20¼ x 32 in.
(51.4 x 81.3 cm)

Soon after his return to the United States and the start of his crucial relationship with Alfred Stieglitz, Arthur Dove began to experiment with abstraction, color, and media, at various times using oil, pastel, wax emulsion, collage, and assemblage. The Museum's pastel *Team of Horses* (1911 or 1912) is an excellent example of Dove's innovative work during this period and contrasts to the more conventional *Lobster* of his European years. *Thunder Shower*, painted near the end of Dove's life, clearly demonstrates the changes in his art after his European explorations. In contrast to *The Lobster* (see preceding plate), the later work is characterized by muted tones, an experimental medium, and a typically modernist subject.

Despite his innovative use of media to render abstract forms, Dove always closely tied his art to the land, the sea, and the natural phenomena he observed. He lived near the ocean for much of his career (even on a boat during the 1920s) and always struggled to supplement his meager income from art through fishing, farming, or commercial illustration. Like the Hudson River School painters of the nineteeth century—albeit by more abstract means—Dove and his fellow modernists, among them Georgia O'Keeffe and the photographer Alfred Stieglitz, sought to capture the fleeting effects of nature's enduring powers.

Dove described one of his earlier works as depicting the "repetitions and convolutions of the rage of the tempest"—an apt characterization for *Thunder Shower*. The painting was inspired by a specific occurrence that Dove recorded in his diaries: a storm on Long Island through which he and his second wife, artist Helen Torr (1886–1967), drove in the fall of 1939. Irregular, jagged forms explode outward from the lightning bolt that divides the image; the whole effectively evokes the powerful vibrations, sounds, and colors of a violent storm.

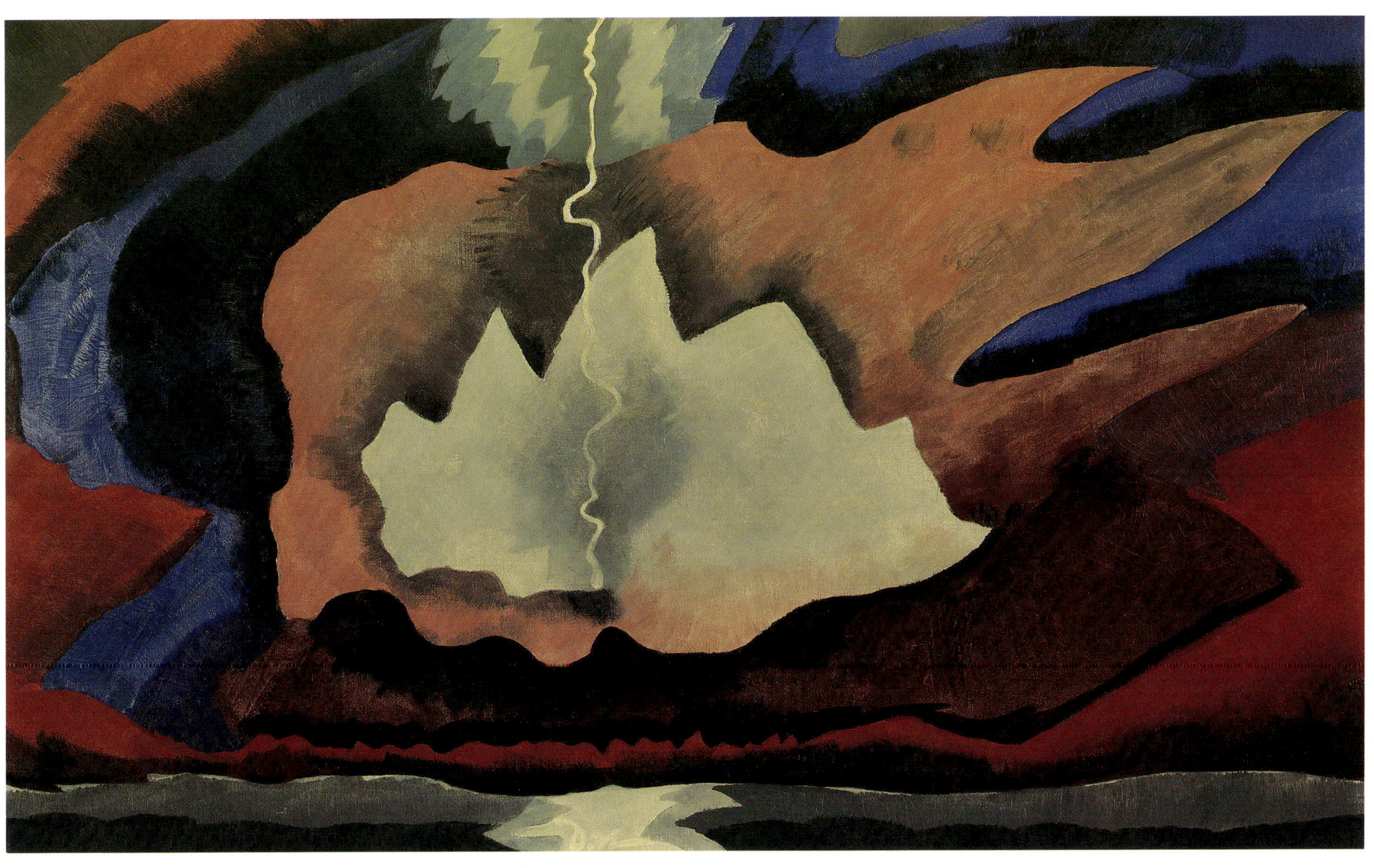

MARSDEN HARTLEY
(1877–1943)

Earth Cooling

1932
Oil on cardboard mounted on Masonite, 24½ x 33⅞ in.
(62.2 x 86.0 cm)

A leading American modernist and a protégé of Alfred Stieglitz, Marsden Hartley traveled almost constantly between various locales in Europe and America and worked in many different styles. Although he had studied under William Merritt Chase at the National Academy of Design, he was more profoundly influenced by the colorful expressionism of artists such as Henri Matisse and Wassily Kandinsky, whose work he was exposed to both at Alfred Stieglitz' 291 Gallery and while traveling and studying in Europe. By 1932, when he painted *Earth Cooling*, the artist had executed landscapes, still lifes, and abstractions inspired by a number of European styles—neo-impressionism, German expressionism, and cubism (seen in the Museum's *Provincetown Abstraction*, 1916)—and by individual artists, notably Matisse, Pablo Picasso, and Paul Cézanne.

In failing health, Hartley went to Mexico in 1932 on a Guggenheim Fellowship. Despite his conviction that the place "devitalized" his energies, he found camaraderie there with writers and other artists, and inspiration in the ancient cultures and light-filled mountainous landscape. While many of his Mexican paintings, such as a 1933 memorial to the poet Hart Crane, were what he called "pictures of just shapes and movements . . . [employed] in the way of symbols," others, such as *Earth Cooling*, are also direct representations of the solid, sculptural forms of his surroundings. The intense reds, browns, yellows, and blues of the simplified forms and the flattened appearance of the background peaks give the painting a somewhat mythic quality. The vibrant red mountain caps; amorphous, lava-like foreground areas; brilliant yellow horizon; and glowing ovoid cloud shapes suggest extreme, pulsating heat and nearly belie the painting's title: only the green-blue sky suggests any sense of cooling. This scene seems more evocative of a primordial, oozing landscape, which Hartley may well have had in mind; during the same trip, he painted the sacred volcano of Popocatepetl.

During the following decade, Hartley continued to employ the expressive style seen in *Earth Cooling*, painting the elemental forms of mountainous landscapes in New England, Nova Scotia, New Mexico, Bermuda, and the Bavarian Alps. The artist also painted a number of still lifes, such as the Museum's *Sombrero and Gloves* of 1936. He returned to his native Maine in 1937 and spent the rest of his life painting that state's rugged terrain and people.

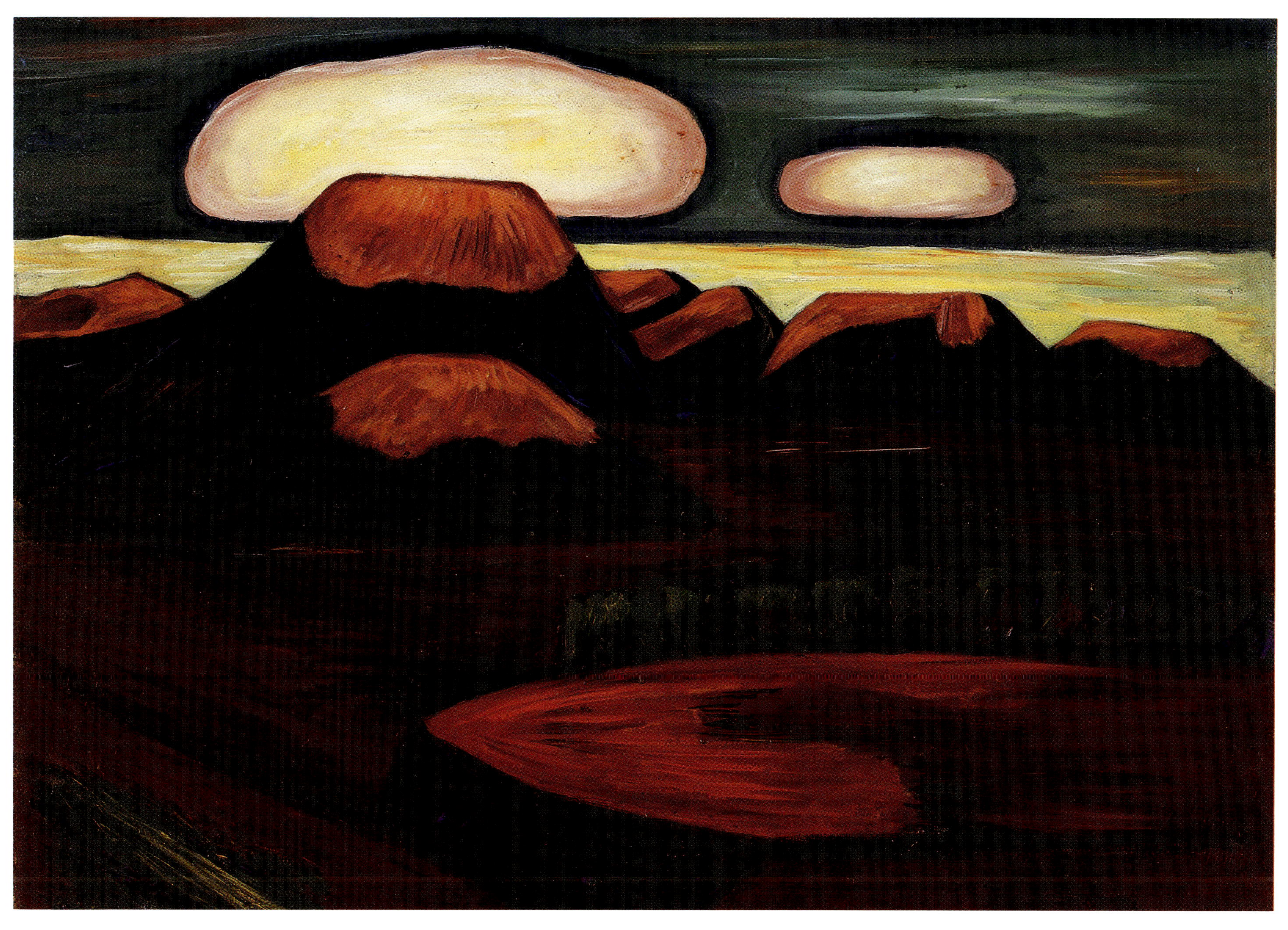

GEORGIA O'KEEFFE
(1887–1986)

Dark Mesa and Pink Sky

1930
Oil on canvas, 16¼ x 30⅜ in.
(41.3 x 77.2 cm)

Georgia O'Keeffe's long and prolific artistic career, her role as wife and model to the influential photographer and dealer Alfred Stieglitz, and her often reclusive existence in her beloved Southwest have earned her nearly mythic stature in the history of twentieth-century American art. O'Keeffe studied art in Chicago and New York, then taught from 1916 to 1918 in Texas, where she produced the Museum's fine series of watercolors, *Light Coming on the Plains I, II,* and *III* (1917). During this period her paintings came to the attention of Stieglitz, who began in 1916 to exhibit them consistently at his galleries. The two married in 1924.

O'Keeffe painted *Dark Mesa and Pink Sky* in 1930, during her second trip to New Mexico. The canvas reflects her reverence for the beautiful southwestern landscape, which had a profound effect on her art. The site represented may well be the low sand hills of the Rio Grande Valley (recent research suggests a specific location a few miles east of Abiquiu). About this region she observed: "It was the shapes of the hills there that fascinated me. The reddish sand hills with the dark mesas behind them. It seemed as though no matter how far you walked you could never get into those dark hills, although I walked great distances." Certainly these ruminations could describe *Dark Mesa and Pink Sky*, in which O'Keeffe has characteristically reduced the layers of desert and mesa to their essential, sculptural forms and blanketed them with rich colors. The image extends beyond the edges of the horizontal canvas onto the painted frame, suggesting the great expanse of the desert landscape; its serenity, beauty, and timelessness inspire quiet contemplation.

O'Keeffe continued to visit New Mexico yearly from her homes in New York City and Lake George until 1949, three years after Stieglitz' death. She then settled permanently in Abiquiu, New Mexico. In 1953, she made her first trip to Europe, and in subsequent years she traveled abroad frequently. Her increasingly abstract work culminated in her largest canvas, the eight-by-twenty-four-foot *Sky Above Clouds IV* of 1965 (Art Institute of Chicago), which was exhibited for the first time in the Amon Carter Museum's 1966 retrospective of her work. O'Keeffe died in Santa Fe, at the age of ninety-nine, in 1986.

The Museum's holdings of the artist's work include another canvas from her 1930 trip, *Ranchos Church-Taos* (see next plate), and *Black Patio Door* (1955), a later work depicting part of her home in Abiquiu. *Red Cannas* (1927) is a masterful example of her well-known flower paintings.

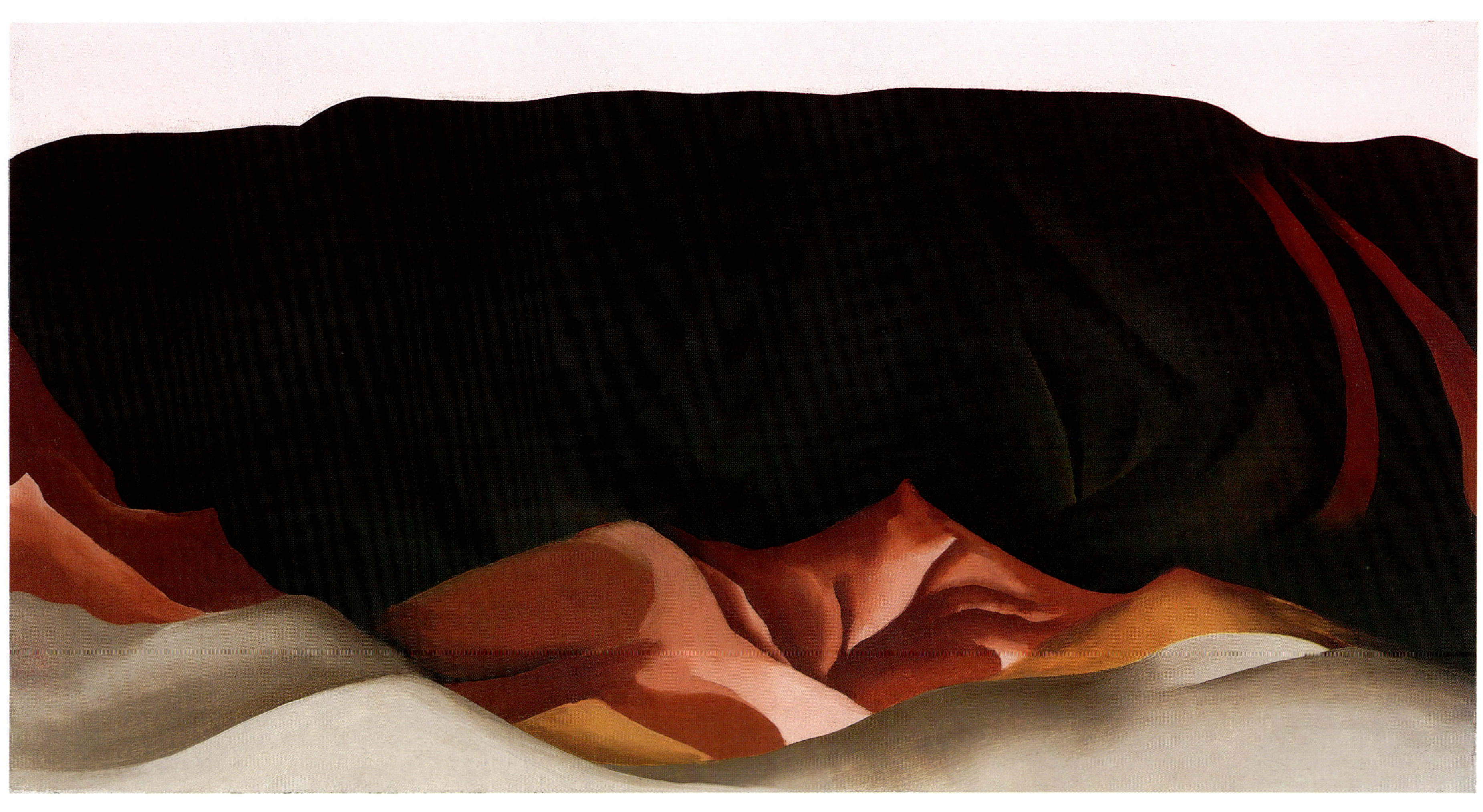

GEORGIA O'KEEFFE

(1887–1986)

Ranchos Church—Taos (Ranch Church—Grey Sky)

1930
Oil on canvas, 24¼ x 36 in.
(61.6 x 91.4 cm)

Like many painters and photographers who have traveled to or lived in New Mexico, Georgia O'Keeffe was inspired to depict the eighteenth-century missionary church of St. Francis of Assisi, located in Ranchos de Taos in the Sangre de Cristo mountains. *Ranchos Church* is one of about eight paintings of the edifice that the artist executed during her first extended visits to New Mexico in the summers of 1929 and 1930 (she had passed through the state briefly on her way to Colorado in 1917). This important group of canvases marks the beginning of O'Keeffe's long mature career, in which she produced numerous images of New Mexico. Although it was not unusual for her to treat one subject repeatedly, undoubtedly the church's adobe construction and its simple, nearly organic forms prompted this concentration. She proclaimed the church "one of the most beautiful buildings left in the United States by the early Spaniards."

Significantly, in all but one image O'Keeffe chose to depict the simple, massive forms of the church's buttressed apse rather than the more complex east entrance with its towers, crosses, and gate. These sculptural, almost abstract shapes appear to grow out of the ground and seem to assume the characteristics of the area's mountains. O'Keeffe's exaggeration of the structure's curves and of the slope of the earth upon which it sits, as well as the nearly monochromatic palette which unites the ground with the church, further likens the structure to a natural formation silhouetted against a cloudy sky. As in many of her landscapes, including *Dark Mesa and Pink Sky* (see preceding plate), O'Keeffe blurs the distinctions between near and far by filling the canvas with her subject, pushing it close to the surface of the picture plane and eliminating any detail or context. *Ranchos Church* confronts the viewer and demands attention as it simultaneously seems to hide and protect from the beholder something sacred within its bulging walls. It is these unique combinations and contrasts—of the inviting and the formidable, the close and distant, the naturalistic and the abstract—that characterize O'Keeffe's most successful New Mexico works, such as *Ranchos Church*.

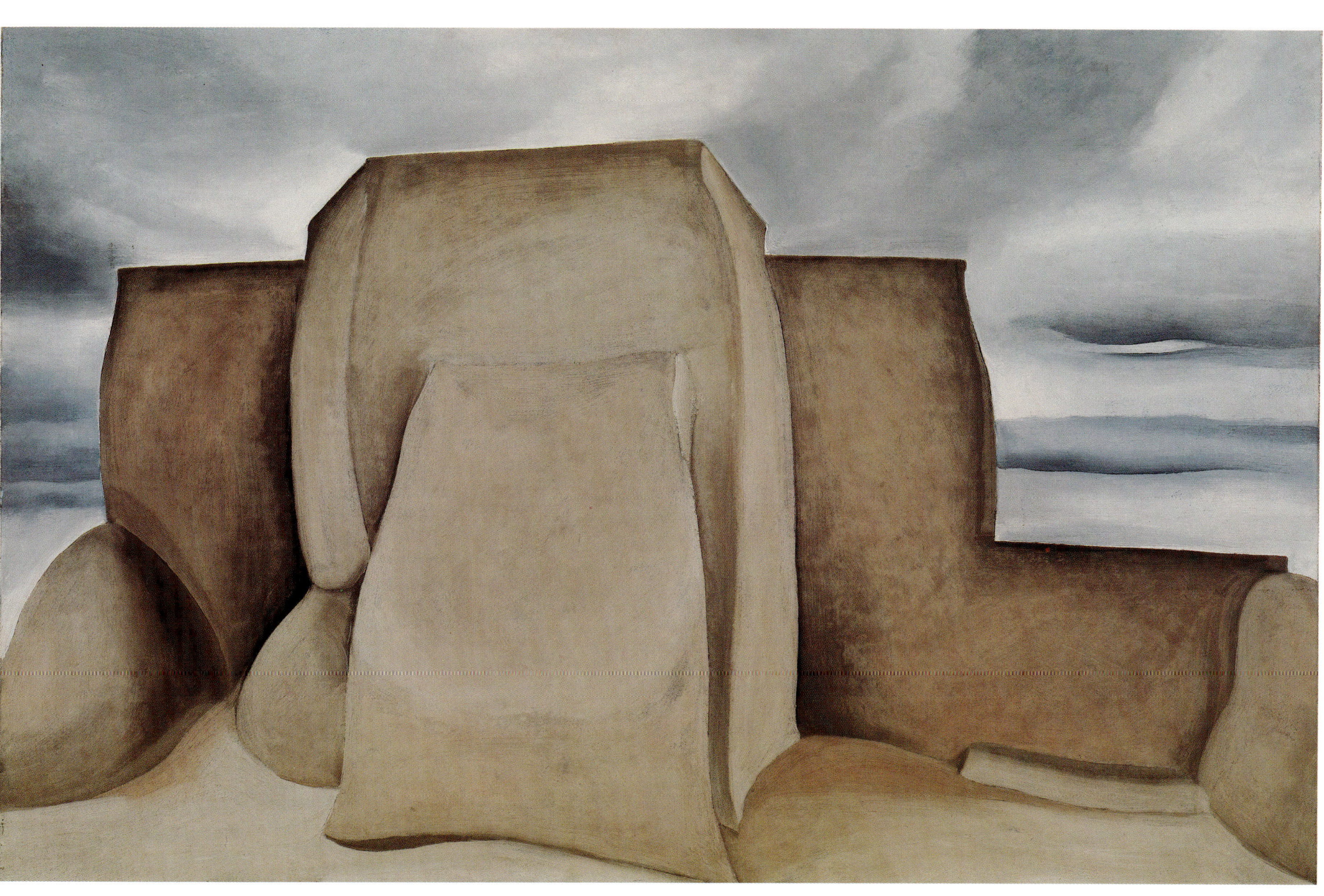

GRANT WOOD
(1891–1942)

Parson Weems' Fable

1939
Oil on canvas, 38⅜ x 50⅛ in.
(97.5 x 127.3 cm)

Grant Wood, John Steuart Curry, and Thomas Hart Benton were the primary exponents of an American Regionalist school of painting, which envisioned "[t]he hope of a native American art in the development of regional art centers and competition among them." After training briefly at the Art Institute of Chicago and as a maker of jewelry and metalwork, Wood studied at Paris' Académie Julien following World War I. Returning to his native Iowa to paint familiar surroundings, he asserted that "all the really good ideas I ever had came to me while I was milking a cow." His famous painting *American Gothic* (1930, Art Institute of Chicago) made him an overnight sensation at age thirty-eight.

Nine years later Wood created another icon of American Regionalism and one of the Museum's most popular paintings, *Parson Weems' Fable*, based on the famous tale of George Washington's youthful honesty. Parson Mason Locke Weems, a bookseller, itinerant preacher, and creator of the cherry tree legend in the fifth edition of his *Life of George Washington* (1806), is shown revealing his story's decisive moment. His pose begins a clever chain of hand gestures that unifies all of the figures and provides the illusion of recession. Echoed by the diagonals of the curtain edge, the house (Wood's own Iowa City home), and the lawn, the gestures conclude with the two slaves who pick cherries from a tree at the upper left. Wood cleverly used other repeating motifs, such as spherical shapes seen in the trees, buttons, cherries, and cherry-like fringes. The artist also designed the painting's frame, which repeats the spherical motif with ornamental beading and picks up the star on the house with a series of painted stars.

Wood's most obvious whimsical touch is his use of the head from Gilbert Stuart's well-known Atheneum portrait to render the young George recognizable. George's slightly worried expression and his father's admonishing one (variations on Weems' characterizations) are also reflected symbolically by the gathering storm clouds.

Although delightfully amusing today, the artist's visual puns and rhythms seemed to Wood's contemporaries to satirize and deride the famous legend. Wood, however, claimed that he actually wished to preserve such folklore, especially at a time when Fascism threatened democracy. In fact, he intended the canvas to be the first in a series of paintings portraying American historical myths; the second painting was to depict his own version of the Pocahontas story, "Capt. John Smith's Rescue of Pocahontas." The group was never realized, due in part to his untimely death three years after the completion of *Parson Weems' Fable*. The few canvases Wood completed during that period repeat the more commonplace subjects of his earlier career: landscapes and scenes of everyday life inspired by his Iowa environs.

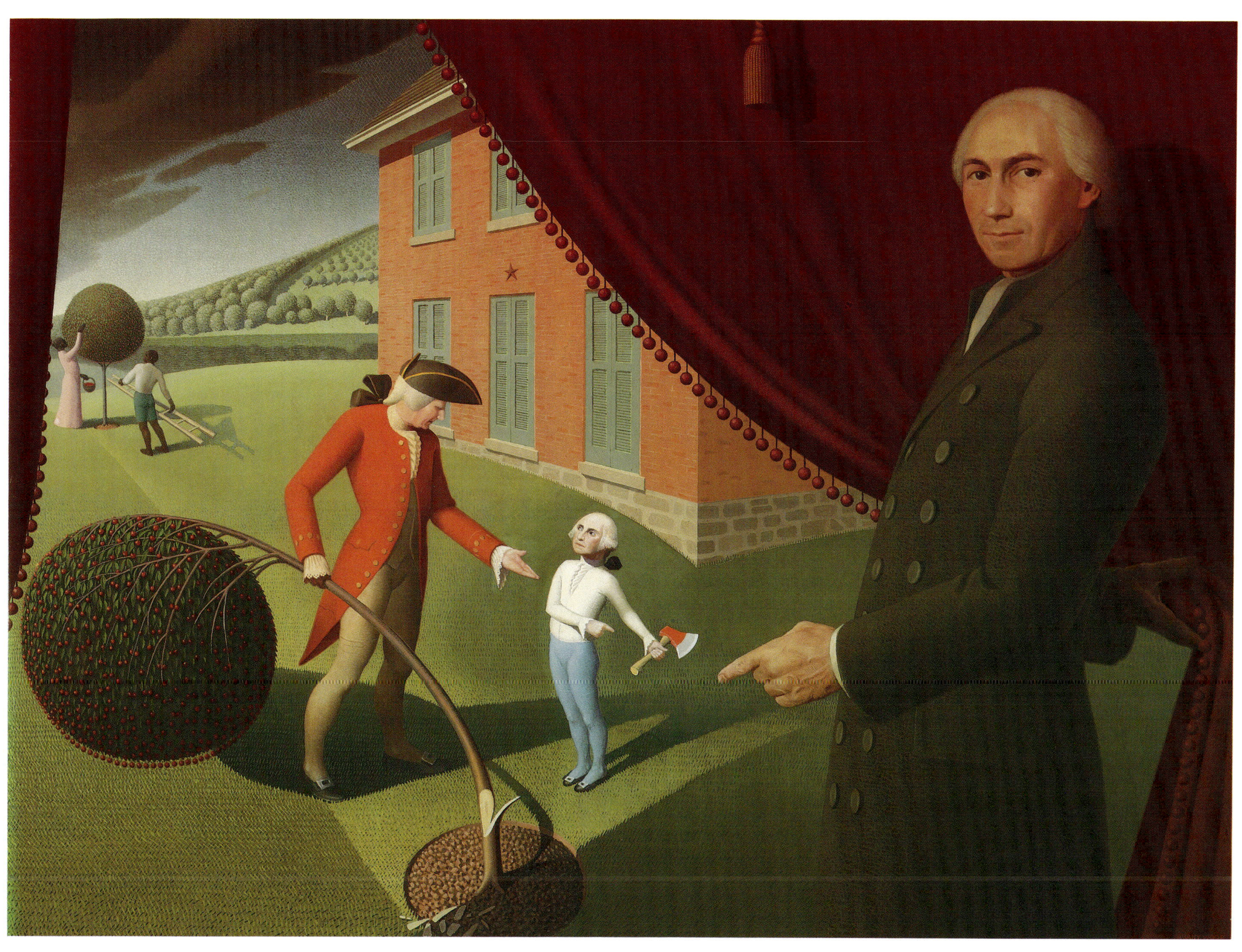

STUART DAVIS
(1892–1964)

Blips and Ifs

1963–64
Oil on canvas, 71⅛ x 53⅛ in.
(180.7 x 134.9 cm)
Acquisition in memory of John de Menil, Trustee, Amon Carter Museum, 1961–1969

Stuart Davis' career as one of America's leading modern artists spanned more than fifty years. His early work is represented in the Museum's collection by his *Self-Portrait* (1919), which was inspired by Van Gogh. However, most of Davis' highly distinctive work transcended changing artistic currents. Consistently characterized by a bright palette and dynamic compositions, his works drew inspiration from the lively sights and sounds of modern American life.

Two important early influences on the Philadelphia-born artist were his study with the famous teacher Robert Henri, who encouraged all his students to "place the origins of art in life," and his exposure to modern European art, especially cubism, first exhibited in America at New York's Armory Show of 1913. "Synthetic" cubism, with its collage-like juxtapositions of broad, flat areas of color separated by thick lines, particularly affected Davis and, in some form or other, is the basis for all of his compositions. Davis traveled to Santa Fe (where he painted the Museum's *New Mexican Landscape*) in 1923 and to Europe in 1928–29, but otherwise he remained in New York, the city that so animated his art.

Blips and Ifs is the last painting Davis completed. Its monumental size, bold abstraction, and bright palette loudly proclaim it as the consummate celebration of the artist's stylistic and thematic concerns. Words, depicted in so many of his earlier works as parts of signs and buildings in the cityscape, are now themselves the collective subject for a painting; it has been proposed that they reflect the artist's growing obsession with the terms of art theory. The fragmentation of the "word-shapes" by the edges of the picture plane gives the canvas the appearance of a detail magnified from an even larger work, and this tension at the canvas' periphery reinforces the explosive effect of the image. The opposition between the blacks and whites and among the reds, greens, and yellows also contributes to the work's highly dynamic quality. The bold, rhythmic abstraction of the work bespeaks the influence not only of New York's frenetic pace, lights, and signs, but also of the "hot" sounds of the jazz music Davis loved. In keeping with his use of words as subject, the artist integrates his own bold signature into the visual excitement of the image.

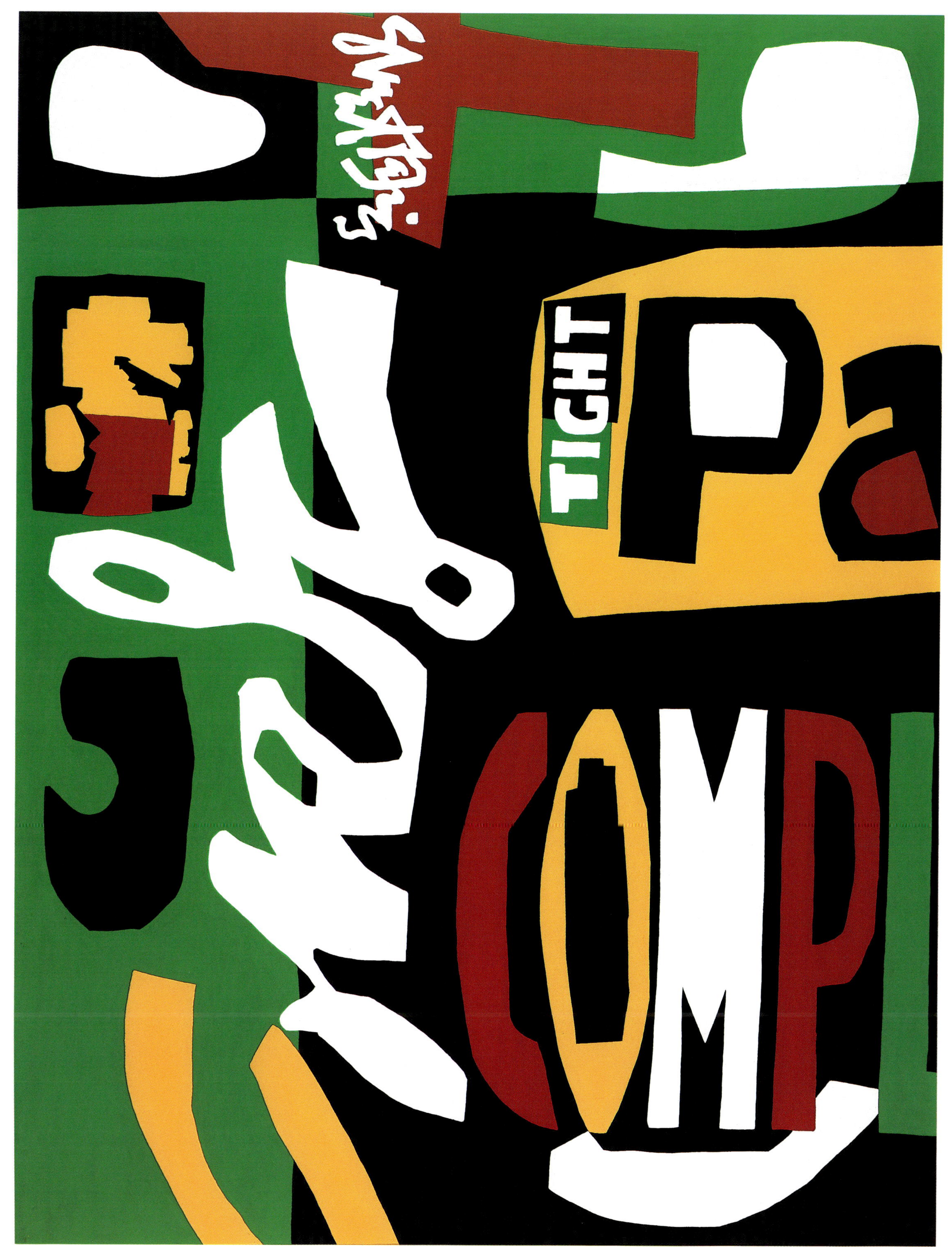

TIGHT
Pa
COMP